Practical Seminar
Simultaneous Interpretation
by Whispering

実践ゼミ

# ウィスパリング

柴田バネッサ 著

# 同時通訳

南雲堂

## Acknowledgements
### for their invaluable suggestions and contributions

| | | |
|---|---|---|
| 水野五行 | Dr. Richard Lions | Joud Jabri-Picket |
| Herman Bartelen | Milton Combs | Caroline Dashtestani |
| Greg O'Dowd | Anton Goodings | Alan Goodman |
| Steve Heverly | Evelyn Janetta | Siobhan Moore |
| Nicholas Walker | Ian Wyness | T. J. Arata |

Thanks to the dedicated support and effort of the following people revisions were possible Prof. Chikako Tsuruta, Manami Sohma, Katsuhiko Hirahara

## はじめに

　一つの言語をマスターするには2000時間が必要だと言われています。このうちの1000時間は学校で学習しているものとして，次の1000時間はリスニングとリピーティングと語彙の定着に重点を置いて，『使える英語』を習得して下さい。

　本書では通訳者トレーニングの手法を応用し，リスニングとリピーティングを中心にウィスパリング（ささやき型同時通訳）スキル習得も狙いに定めてあります。ウィスパリングの練習過程でボランティア通訳Ａ級取得が射程距離に入って来るでしょう。ウィスパリングは難しいものではありません。まずは英文パターンが自然に口から出るようになることに目標をおいて練習をはじめて下さい。

　本書はリスニング・スピーキング力をアップしたい人から，日本商工会議所の英語ビジネス通訳者認定試験の一般クラスの受験を目指す人までを対象としています。本書のトレーニングを，新聞，雑誌，その他の素材を用いて学習に応用して下さい。学習進度の目安は１週間で１レッスンです。

# 目　次

はじめに　3
アプローチ　9
本書のトレーニング構成と練習方法　11

**Lesson 1**　§1　クイック・レスポンス　16
　　　　　　§2　リテンションとリプロダクション　17
　　　　　　§3　区切り聞き　18
　　　　　　§4　通訳基本練習　Shopping　20
　　　　　　§5　頭ごなし訳練習　24

**Lesson 2**　§1　クイック・レスポンス　26
　　　　　　§2　リテンションとリプロダクション　27
　　　　　　§3　区切り聞き　28
　　　　　　§4　通訳基本練習　Food　30
　　　　　　§5　サイト・トランスレーションとリテイン処理　32

**Lesson 3**　§1　クイック・レスポンス　34
　　　　　　§2　リテンションとリプロダクション　35
　　　　　　§3　区切り聞き　36
　　　　　　§4　通訳基本練習　Weather　38
　　　　　　§5　通訳メモ　41

**Lesson 4**　§1　クイック・レスポンス　44
　　　　　　§2　リテンションとリプロダクション　45
　　　　　　§3　区切り聞き　46

　　　　　　§4　通訳基本練習　Travel　　48
　　　　　　§5　商談通訳　接待1　　50

**Lesson 5**　§1　クイック・レスポンス　　52
　　　　　　§2　リテンションとリプロダクション　　53
　　　　　　§3　区切り聞き　　54
　　　　　　§4　商談通訳　接待2　　56
　　　　　　§5　ディクテーション　　58

**Lesson 6**　§1　クイック・レスポンス　　60
　　　　　　§2　リテンションとリプロダクション　　61
　　　　　　§3　区切り聞き　　62
　　　　　　§4　商談通訳　接待3　　64
　　　　　　§5　ディクテーション　　66

**Lesson 7**　§1　クイック・レスポンス　　68
　　　　　　§2　リテンションとリプロダクション　　69
　　　　　　§3　区切り聞き　　70
　　　　　　§4　通訳基本練習　Sports　　73
　　　　　　§5　ディクテーション　　74

**Lesson 8**　§1　クイック・レスポンス　　76
　　　　　　§2　リテンションとリプロダクション　　77
　　　　　　§3　区切り聞き　　78
　　　　　　§4　商談通訳　情報提供　　79
　　　　　　§5　速読練習　ボナペ　　83

**Lesson 9**　§1　クイック・レスポンス　　84

　　　　　　　§2　リテンションとリプロダクション　　85
　　　　　　　§3　区切り聞き　　86
　　　　　　　§4　商談通訳　質問　　88
　　　　　　　§5　ディクテーション　相撲　　90

Lesson 10　§1　クイック・レスポンス　　92
　　　　　　　§2　リテンションとリプロダクション　　93
　　　　　　　§3　区切り聞き　　94
　　　　　　　§4　商談通訳　値引き交渉1　　96
　　　　　　　§5　速読またはサイトラ練習　イラン　　98

Lesson 11　§1　クイック・レスポンス　　100
　　　　　　　§2　リテンションとリプロダクション　　101
　　　　　　　§3　区切り聞き　　102
　　　　　　　§4　商談通訳　値引き交渉2　　104
　　　　　　　§5　速読またはサイトラ練習　　106

Lesson 12　§1　クイック・レスポンス　　108
　　　　　　　§2　リテンションとリプロダクション　　109
　　　　　　　§3　区切り聞き　　110
　　　　　　　§4　ウィスパリング商談通訳　プレゼン　　112
　　　　　　　§5　メモ化リプロダクション　宗教　　114
　　　　　　　§6　要約通訳　モラ氏歓送会　　115

Lesson 13　§1　クイック・レスポンス　　116
　　　　　　　§2　リテンションとリプロダクション　　117
　　　　　　　§3　区切り聞き　　118
　　　　　　　§4　商談通訳　労働関係　　120

　　　　　　§5　メモ化リプロダクション　庭園　122
　　　　　　§6　サイトラ原稿付き同時通訳　バレンタイン　123

**Lesson 14**　§1　クイック・レスポンス　124
　　　　　　§2　リテンションとリプロダクション　125
　　　　　　§3　区切り聞き　126
　　　　　　§4　商談通訳　サマリー　128
　　　　　　§5　リプロダクション　結婚　130
　　　　　　§6　簡単な同時通訳　131

**Lesson 15**　§1　クイック・レスポンス　132
　　　　　　§2　リテンションとリプロダクション　133
　　　　　　§3　区切り聞き　134
　　　　　　§4　メモ取り要約通訳　討議　136
　　　　　　§5　通訳基本練習　着物　138

**Lesson 16**　§1　クイック・レスポンス　140
　　　　　　§2　リテンションとリプロダクション　141
　　　　　　§3　区切り聞き　142
　　　　　　§4　ウィスパリング同時商談通訳　合弁計画　144
　　　　　　§5　通訳基本練習　皇居　146

**Lesson 17**　§1　クイック・レスポンス　148
　　　　　　§2　リテンションとリプロダクション　149
　　　　　　§3　区切り聞き　150
　　　　　　§4　商談通訳　価格交渉　152
　　　　　　§5　通訳基本練習　浅草　154

**Lesson 18**　§1　クイック・レスポンス　　156
　　　　　　　§2　リテンションとリプロダクション　　157
　　　　　　　§3　区切り聞き　　158
　　　　　　　§4　芸能ウィスパリング通訳　女優　　160

**Lesson 19**　§1　クイック・レスポンス　　164
　　　　　　　§2　リテンションとリプロダクション　　165
　　　　　　　§3　区切り聞き　　166
　　　　　　　§4　芸能ウィスパリング通訳　格闘技選手　　168

**Lesson 20**　§1　クイック・レスポンス　　172
　　　　　　　§2　リテンションとリプロダクション　　173
　　　　　　　§3　区切り聞き　　174
　　　　　　　§4　芸能ウィスパリング通訳　ミュージシャン　　176

ワン・センテンス遅れ通訳ウォーミング・アップ　　180
簡単な同時通訳　　189

## アプローチ

『使える英語力』を持つためには，自分のレベルに合った文章を自分のレベルに合ったスピードで聞き，**実際にスピードがつくまで繰り返して発音する**ことです。リスニングを中心に耳から英語をインプットします。これにより英語的感覚を養います。

本書のトレーニングは5つのセクションから成っています。
　　セクション1は語彙のクイック・レスポンス，
　　セクション2は英語のセンテンス・リピーティング，
　　セクション3は英語の区切り聞き，
　　セクション4は日英通訳練習，
　　セクション5が，その他の技能訓練です。
　　進度の目安は1レッスンにつき1週間です。

## 学習の目標

### ◎第1目標

　一分間に160ワードのスピードで一般的な文章を音読しながら理解できるようにする。（これがリスニング力アップのポイントです。）同じ素材を何回も繰り返して音読し，リーディング・スピードを上げていきます。一分間に160ワードを聞き取れるようになりたい人は，同素材を一分間に160ワードで読みきれるまで音読練習します。
　分速150から160ワードはネイティブ同士が自然に会話を行うときの『ナチュラル・スピード』です。リーディング・スピードが160 wpm あれば，リスニングが非常に楽になるはずです。

◎第2目標
　ボランティア通訳検定のA級取得，TOEICリスニング50点アップ
◎第3目標
　同時通訳入門レベルを修了　分速110ワード±20のスピーチを初見で70％以上同時通訳できる。分速150±10ワードのスピーチを聞き逐次通訳用のメモ取りができる。通訳技能検定の2級取得
◎第4目標
　同時通訳中級レベルを修了　分速140±20ワードのスピーチを聞き，初見で60％以上ウィスパリング同時通訳できる。
　日本商工会議所の英語ビジネス通訳者認定試験の一般クラス上位合格

**参考**

| 資　格 | 主　催 |
|---|---|
| ボランティア通訳検定B級 | 日本通訳協会　03-3209-4741 |
| 　英検準2級（TOEIC 470）程度 | |
| ボランティア通訳検定A級 | 日本通訳協会 |
| 　英検準1級（TOEIC 700）程度 | センテンス逐次通訳技能が必須 |
| 通訳技能検定2級 | 日本通訳協会 |
| 　英検1級　（TOEIC 800）程度 | 長文逐次のためメモ取り技能が必須 |
| 英語ビジネス通訳者認定試験 | 日本商工会議所　03-3402-2109 |
| 日本経済新聞の一面経済・国際面（日英・英日）から出題される。 | |
| 　英検1級程度 | 商談関係の語彙とメモ取り技能が必須 |
| 　　一次試験 | 英語力とビジネス知識 |
| 　　二次試験　通訳技能 | 日英・英日の訳出テープ吹込み，（メモを取りながら通訳） |

　因みに，選択技能検定の二次試験の合格者は三次試験を受けることができます。
　三次試験は日英・英日のオーディション方式実演です。

# 本書のトレーニング構成と練習方法

### §1　クイック・レスポンス　　目的：即時訳出とボキャビル
1　英語と日本語を同時に一語として覚える練習をする。
2　口頭で即時変換練習をする　　　　日英，英日
3　リストの語彙を読み上げてもらい，一語遅れの即時変換練習をする。
　　日英，英日

### §2　リテンションとリピーティング　　目的：情報保持
1　数回音読して暗唱する。
2　うまくいかなかったところを原稿で確認し，重点的に練習する。
3　日本語文を見て全文がリプロデュースできるまで練習する。

### §3　区切り聞きとリピーティング　　目的：プロソディー分析，
　　　　　　　　　　　　　　　　　　　　　　訳出セグメントの判断

　素材は自由課題のものでよく，どのレベルでも，スクリプトがあれば，分速160ワード以上のものを使用してもよいでしょう。自分が通訳を始めると思う部分で区切ります。
1　録音された英語のマテリアルを通して聞く。
2　素材を区切り聞きし，おうむ返しのリピーティング練習する。
3　区切り聞きしながら，同じ箇所の日本語の訳文を音読する。
4　区切り聞きしながら，自分の言葉で通訳する。
5　全パッセージを通して聞きサイレント・シャドーイングする。（文を聞きながら1～3語遅れて輪唱するようについて行く。）

注：本書のカセットと素材の区切れの個所は一致しません。意味のまとまりごとに各自の判断でリピーティングと通訳を工夫して下さい。

## §4　通訳基本練習

### (1)　日英通訳練習　　目的：即時訳出

1　日本文を読み口頭で英訳する。
2　日本語文を聞き英語で逐次通訳する。旨く通訳できなかったところをチェックし再度練習する。
3　次に同じ日本語文をワン・センテンスずつ聞きながらできるところから同時通訳してみる。（各センテンスの後に2～3秒のポーズを入れておくと練習しやすい。）

### (2)　ワン・センテンス遅れ通訳　　目的：口と耳との分離作業

1　日英通訳練習の1-3の手順に引き続き練習をしてから，最終的には通常のスピーチのように自然なテンポで文章を読み上げ，ワン・センテンス遅れで訳出をする。
2　長めのセンテンスは和文を切りのよいところで細切れにし，内容の予測をしながら文をつないでゆく練習をする。

## §5　その他の主要トレーニング

### (1)　サイト・トランスレーション　　目的：即時訳出，長文読解力

目で文章を追いながら口頭で訳出します。なるべく文頭から『頭ごなし訳』にしますが，目で先に読み進んでいける範囲では後ろから訳し上げてもかまいません。『頭ごなし訳』のテクニックは『はじめてのウィスパリング同時通訳』（1997，南雲堂）を参照して下さい。

### (2)　ウィスパリング同時通訳　　目的：即時訳出，口と耳との分離作業

『ウィスパリング』とはスピーチを聞いてささやき声で同時通訳を行っていく方法です。そのトレーニング方法は，通常の同時通訳訓練と同じです。
1　全文を通して聞く。
2　全文を聞きながら，モデル訳に目を通す。
3　出来るところから同時通訳する。

4　最後にテープに録音しながら同時通訳する。

(3)　**メモ取りと要約通訳**　目的：情報保持と処理

　聞きながら手が動き，後にメモが判読できるようにするのが目標です。
1　スクリプトをもとに主要部分をメモ化してみる。
2　テープをかけてスピーチを聞きながらメモをとる。
3　メモを見てスピーチを口頭要約します。全体の1/3位の長さにする。

## §6　"内容の先取り予測"のための学習

　スピーチを聞いて"内容の先取り予測"をするためには，背景知識の学習が重要です。通訳の技能検定試験や認定試験を考える場合，政治，経済，労働問題，工業英語，国際問題等からの出題を想定して"対策"をたてます。

**課題1**　自分が日常日本語で話していることはどのようなことでしょうか。リストアップしてみて下さい。最もよく使っている200表現を選び英語にして暗記して下さい。なお，現時点ですでに使いこなせるものは数に入れません。英語と日本語がどちらにも即時に転換できるまで口頭練習します。

**課題2**　世界の一か国を選び，その国の歴史，政治経済等を調べ，英語でプレゼンテーションをすると想定してスピーチを書いて下さい。

**課題3**　ニュース，ドキュメンタリー，インタビュー等を英訳し，時事英語の語彙を学習して下さい。

**課題4**　日本経済新聞の一面をサイトラして下さい。　英日，日英

**課題5**　英文契約書とその訳出例を調べ，法律用語を学習して下さい。テキストとしては市販の翻訳本等を使用します。

**課題6**　外国人研修生の一団をエスコートし自動車製造工場を見学する場合を想定して，製造の過程を調べ，英訳して下さい。
　通常，通訳は無線のマイクを手に持ち説明しながら引率します。

**課題7**　環境問題を協議する国際会議のシナリオを書いて下さい。

## 実践ゼミ
## ウィスパリング同時通訳

# Lesson 1

## §1 クイック・レスポンス〔QR〕

(1) ボキャビル

**演習方法**

日本語と英語を同時に一語として覚える練習をします。

"商品—merchandise"のように日英合成語にして数回ずつ発音して下さい。一合成語を2秒以内で発音します。

## Shopping & Asia is close 1

| | | |
|---|---|---|
| 1 | 商品 | merchandise |
| 2 | 物 | goods |
| 3 | 消費税 | consumption tax |
| 4 | 保証 | guarantee |
| 5 | 露店 | stall |
| 6 | 交渉する | bargain |
| 7 | 商品をながめる | browse |
| 8 | 選ぶ | select |
| 9 | つけにする | charge |
| 10 | 手頃な | reasonable |
| 11 | 安い | economical／inexpensive |
| 12 | 月賦で | by (*or* in) installments |
| 13 | 返金 | refund |
| 14 | 追放された王子 | an exiled prince |
| 15 | 砦 | fortress |
| 16 | アジアが好き | Asianphile |
| 17 | 建てられた | It was founded |
| 18 | 形式ばらない | casual |
| 19 | オランダ | the Netherlands |
| 20 | 負ける | be defeated |

(2) **数字**　英語に変換して下さい。

5千, 1万, 6万, 16万, 10万, 1万, 5万, 8万,
1万5千, 3万8千, 12万, 23万, 30万, 3万, 9千,
33万9千, 52万, 8千, 52万8千, 52万, 7千, 52万7千

## §2　リテンションとリプロダクション

(1) **リテンション練習**　文章全体を覚えていくための練習。
数回音読して暗唱して下さい。　　　　　　　　

A  I'd like to invite you to see our factory while you are in Tokyo.
B  That's very nice of you. But I'm afraid my schedule is full all next week.
A  I'm sorry to hear that. Then maybe next time.
B  Well, anyway this has been a valuable experience for me.
A  It was nice meeting you. I hope we can get together again, soon.

(2) **リプロダクション**
日本語文を読み，または聞いて，即時に訳出して下さい。

A  東京にご滞在の間に当社の工場にお招きしたいと思います。
B  それはどうもご親切に。しかし残念ですが，来週はスケジュールが詰まっているのです。
A  そうでしたか。では次回にしましょう。
B  さてと，とにかく今回の経験は有意義なものでした。
A  お会いできてよかったです。またすぐお会いできることを願っています。

## §3 区切り聞き

**演習方法**

初回の区切り聞きではリピーティング，二回目は該当部の日本語訳を音読して下さい。三回目から自分の言葉で通訳して下さい。

最後にサイレント・シャドーイングして達成度をチェックします。

CDは各自が訳出の部分を判断して区切り，訳文は参考例より自然なものに仕上げて下さい。

### Asia is close 1

1-2　Milton Combs

| | |
|---|---|
| One of the things I like about | 一つ好きなことがあります |
| Japan is that | 日本は |
| the rest of Asia | その他のアジアの国々が |
| isn't so far away. | 余り遠くないのです。 |
| I have met | 私は |
| a number of Asianphiles | 多くのアジアが好きな人々に |
| and although I have never | 出会いましたが，私自身が |
| considered myself one | そうだと感じたことはありません, |
| I am certainly moving | でもだんだんそうなっている |
| in that direction. | ようです。 |
| The more of Asia | アジアを |
| I experience | 見れば見るほど |
| the more I come to love it. | 好きになるのです。 |
| I recently visited Malaysia | 最近マレーシアに |
| for the first time. | 初めて行きました。 |
| I didn't stay long | 長くは滞在しませんでしたが |
| but enough to | 十分に, |
| fall in love with it. | そこが好きになったのです。 |
| The people were casual | 人々は気さくで |
| and there was that same energy | 同じエネルギーがありました |
| that I find everywhere in Asia. | アジア中にどこにもあるものです。 |

| | |
|---|---|
| In Malaysia | マレーシアでは |
| I visited Malacca, | マラッカという |
| a historical city | 歴史的な町に行きました。 |
| on the southern west coast | 場所は南西海岸です， |
| of peninsular Malaysia. | マレー半島の。 |
| It was founded by | 建設は |
| an exiled prince from Sumatra | スマトラから追放された王子が |
| in 1400. | したもので，1400年でした。 |
| In 1511 it fell to | 1511年に |
| the hands of the Portuguese, | ポルトガルの手に落ち |
| followed by the Dutch in 1641 | ついで1641年にオランダに |
| and then was given to | 後 |
| the British in 1795 | 1795年にはイギリスに |
| to prevent it from | これは |
| falling to the French | フランスに渡らないように |
| | 取られた措置でした。 |
| when the Netherlands | この時オランダがフランスに |
| were defeated by the French. | 負けたからです。 |
| "Afomosa" a fortress | アフォモーサは砦で |
| which I visited was | 私が訪れたのですが |
| built by the Portuguese | ポルトガル人に建設され， |
| only 19 years after | そのわずか19年前に |
| Columbus discovered the | コロンブスがアメリカ大陸を発見し |
| Americas which, | ており， |
| from an American view, | これは，アメリカ人としては |
| goes back to | |
| the beginning of our history. | 歴史の始まりの頃です。 |

## §4　通訳基本練習

### (1)　日英通訳練習
**演習方法**
1　日本語文を読みまたは聞き，英語文を音読します。
2　日本語文を読みまたは聞き，英語で逐次通訳し，うまくできなかった箇所の解答例を確認し重点的に練習します。
3　次に同じ日本語文をワン・センテンスごとに，目で読みながら，または聞きながら，出来るところから同時通訳します。

### 買い物

1　私は買い物に行くのが好きです。
2　私は一番安いものを買うことにしています。
3　私はよく駅のキオスクで買い物をします。
4　私はアクセサリーを買うのが好きです。
5　私は最高級のダイヤを買いました。
6　私はいつもよく考えてから買い物をします。
7　私はいつも家に帰る途中でディスカウント・ストアに寄ります。
8　釣り銭のいらないようにお願いします。
9　コンピュータを買うためにお金を貯めています。
10　午後7時を過ぎると生鮮食品は半額です。
11　5万円持っていたらいいのになあ。(持っていない。)
12　私の母が買い物をします。
13　母は値切るのが上手です。
14　兄は買い物をするのが大嫌いです。面倒なのだそうです。
15　この頃はカタログ・ショッピングをよく利用します。
16　姉は衝動買いする質です。
17　大きな物を買うときはクレジット・カードを使います。
18　骨とう品を買うときは祖母に相談します。
19　兄は車を月賦で買いました。
20　内金を払って，取り置きしていただくのは可能でしょうか。

## 英日通訳練習

### 演習方法

即時変換練習を行って下さい。

## Shopping

1 I like going shopping.
2 I make it a point to buy the least expensive things.
3 I often shop at station kiosks.
4 I enjoy shopping for accessories.
5 I bought a diamond of superior quality.
6 I'm a careful shopper.
7 I usually drop in at a discount store on the way home.
8 Exact change, please.
9 I've been saving to buy a computer.
10 After 7:00 pm most fresh products are 50% off.
11 I wish I had 50,000 yen.
12 My mother does the shopping.
13 My mother is good at bargaining.
14 My brother hates shopping, he says it's troublesome.
15 These days, I often make use of catalog shopping.
16 My sister is an impulsive buyer.
17 I use credit cards when I purchase large things.
18 When I buy an antique, I consult with my grandmother.
19 My brother bought a car in monthly installments.
20 With a down payment, can I ask you to keep it?

## (2) ワン・センテンス遅れ通訳練習

**演習方法**

1. 日本語文を読みまたは聞き英語で逐次通訳します。うまく通訳出来なかったところを，解答例を参考にして再度訳します。
2. 同じ日本語文全文をゆっくりしたスピードで通して聞きながら，できるところから同時通訳します。実際にはワン・センテンス遅れの訳出をするつもりで練習して下さい。
3. 長めの文は区切りのよいところで切り，内容の予測をしながら文をつないでいくようにします。

### 買い物

ショッピング・センターで買い物するのは楽しいものです。特に宝石を買うのが好きです。でも宝石にそんなにお金をかけられるわけではないのですから，ふつうは見るだけです。でも本当に気に入ったものがあって値段も手頃ならば買います。

　この頃はクレジット・カードが使える所がふえて非常に便利になりました。しかしつい買い過ぎてあとでローンの支払いに悩まされないように気を付けなければなりません。

　大型のディスカウント・ストアでは最新のファッションから電気製品などの品揃えが豊富です。
　私はたいてい日曜日に買い物に出ます。何か買おうと思ったときは，同じ物がほかの店でもっと安く売っていないかどうか確認するようにしています。新聞広告を良くチェックして，衝動買いをしないようにしています。

# 英文スピーチ

### 演習方法
即時変換練習を行って下さい。

## Shopping　　🎧1-4

　It's fun to shop at shopping centers. I particularly like shopping for jewelry. Of course I can't spend very much on jewelry, so usually I just look. But if I really like something and the price is right, I buy it.

　These days we can use credit cards at so many places. It has become very convenient to shop. However not paying attention, we may end up buying so much that we can be burdened with loan payments. So we have to be careful.

　At large discount stores there are wide selections of goods from the latest fashions to electrical appliances. I usually go shopping on Sundays.
　When I think of buying something, I try to see if other stores have the same thing at a cheaper price. Checking newspaper ads well, I make it a point to not make purchases impulsively.

## §5　頭ごなし訳

　文頭から英語のシンタックスにしたがって訳す『頭ごなし訳』を以下の例文で検討して下さい。時には内容を意訳する必要があることも確認して下さい。

**prevent**　　The storm prevented us from reaching the destination.
　　　　　　　　嵐のため　　　　　　　目的地に着けなかった。
　　　　　　We couldn't prevent the virus from spreading.
　　　　　　　　未然に防ぐことができず，ウイルスが広がってしまった。

**derive**　　We derive pleasure from taking care of animals.
　　　　　　　　大いに楽しんでいます。動物の世話をするのを。
　　　　　　Those words derive from Latin.
　　　　　　　　その語の起源はラテン語にある。

**despite**　　Despite the order from the Mayor, the workers didn't leave the site.
　　　　　　　　市長は命令を出したが，労働者は現場に残っていた。
　　　　　　In spite of bad weather, he kept on driving.
　　　　　　　　ひどい天候だったが，運転し続けたのだった。

**except that**　　He is a good man except that he often forgets his promises.
　　　　　　　　彼はいい人なのです，但し約束をちょいちょい忘れるのが玉に傷です。

**successful**　　Successful business negotiation requires a lot of preparation and consideration.
　　　　　　　　商談を成功させるのに必要なことは色々な準備と配慮だ。

## 頭ごなし訳練習

### 演習方法

英語の文章を読み，読んだところから順次に訳します。
なるべく自然な日本語にするためには一字一句全部を訳出する
必要はないということを念頭において訳して下さい。

　例　I'll go to the party, unless it rains heavily.
　　　パーティーには行くつもりです。ただし大雨の場合は別です。

1　The only available rehearsal time was early in the morning or between shows.

2　I would like to mention here that riding a bicycle through Tokyo is safe.

3　One of the biggest dangers is a parked car opening a door in front of you.

4　Just after sitting down at the dinner table, my brother and father had a loud argument peppered with a lot of slang and very colorful language.

### 頭ごなし訳　解答例

1　リハーサル時間として利用出来るのは午前中かショーとショーの合間でした。
2　ここで述べたいのは，東京で自転車に乗って回るのは安全だということです。
3　最も危いことの一つに駐車した車のドアが目の前で開くことがあります。
4　食卓についてから，兄と父が大声で議論しました。その中でスラングと極めて乱暴な言葉が多く使われました。

# Lesson 2

## §1 クイック・レスポンス

(1) ボキャビル

**演習方法**

日本語と英語の合成語を2秒以内で発音して意味を確認します。次に日本語から英語，英語から日本語へ即時変換して下さい。

### Food & Asia is close 2

| | | |
|---|---|---|
| 1 | 栄養 | nutrition |
| 2 | お茶菓子 | refreshments |
| 3 | 乳製品 | dairy products |
| 4 | 肉を切る | carve |
| 5 | 蒸す | steam |
| 6 | とける | melt |
| 7 | かきまわす | stir |
| 8 | 味噌 | bean paste |
| 9 | 納豆 | fermented bean |
| 10 | 蒲鉾 | fish paste |
| 11 | 魚の薫製 | smoked fish |
| 12 | 大根おろし | grated radish |
| 13 | ワサビ | horseradish |
| 14 | 材料 | ingredient |
| 15 | 料理法 | recipe |
| 16 | 青果物 | produce |
| 17 | 最大限に働く | strain |
| 18 | 自転車のペダルを踏む | pedal |
| 19 | 輪タク | trishaw |
| 20 | 灼熱の太陽 | blistering sun |

(2) **数字** 英語に変換して下さい。

7万, 5千, 7万5千, 11万, 21万, 8万, 3千,
8万3千, 21万, 22万, 62万, 4千, 62万4千

## §2 リテンションとリプロダクション

(1) **リテンション練習**
数回音読して暗唱して下さい。 1-6

A　Hi, I'm Meg Kudo of Kanda Tech. I have an appointment with Mr. Han at the Human Resources Center.
B　I see Mr. Han has just stepped out. But he should be back in a short while. Why don't you have a seat.
A　Thank you, but in this case, I think I should go to see Mr. Volca, the chief of the accounting department to hand in this document. I'll be back in 5 minutes.
B　Well, I don't think Mr. Volca is in his office, either. I heard he's absent because he fell last night and hurt his lower back.

(2) **リプロダクション**
日本語文を読み、または聞き、即時に訳出して下さい。

A　こんにちは神田テックの工藤メグです。人材センターのハンさんとお約束があるのですが。
B　そうですか。ハンはちょうど今出たところなのですが。すぐ戻るはずです。どうぞおかけ下さい。
A　どうも、でもこの場合、経理課長のボルカさんにお会いしてこの書類をお渡ししてきましょう。5分で戻ります。
B　あの、ボルカさんもオフィスにいないと思います。
お休みだそうですよ。昨晩転んで腰を痛めたとのことです。

## §3　区切り聞き

**演習方法**

初回の区切り聞きでリピーティング，二回目は該当部の日本語訳を音読し，三回目から自分の言葉で通訳して下さい。最後にシャドーイングをして達成度をチェックします。

### Asia is close 2

| | |
|---|---|
| Life in Malaysia is | マレーシアの生活は |
| a little different. | ちょっと違っています。 |
| I took a bus from Singapore | 私はシンガポールからバスに |
| to Malacca and | 乗りマラッカに行き |
| as I got off the bus and had | バスを降り |
| not taken more than 2 steps | 二歩もいかないうちに |
| a man was in my face | 男が私の目の前に |
| showing me pictures | 写真を見せていました |
| of a place to stay. | 宿泊施設の。 |
| I briefly looked at them | 私はちょっとそれを見 |
| and he handed me a | 彼は私に |
| 1-page information brochure. | パンフレットをよこしました。 |
| "Nice place. You can see." | 「いいとこだよ。わかるだろ。」 |
| Actually, the pictures | 事実，写真は |
| did look nice but I told him | よく見えましたが私は |
| I wanted to walk around before | 歩いてから決めると |
| I decided. | 言いました。 |
| As I started to walk away | 歩き始めると |
| a man who was around 70 | 70歳くらいの男が |
| pedaling a trishaw | 輪タクをこぎながら |
| came up to me and | やって来て |
| told me to get in. | 私に乗るように言いました。 |
| I got in. | 私は乗り込みました。 |

| | |
|---|---|
| Not being an experienced traveler | 旅慣れた旅行者ではないので |
| I didn't discuss the price, | 値段の交渉をしませんでした。 |
| which I came to learn | 後にわかったのですが |
| should be done first, | それは初めにするべきことで |
| preferably on a time basis. | 時間制がいいのです。 |
| I asked for his name. | 私は彼に名前を聞きました。 |
| He was Mr. Ong, | 彼はオングさんでした。 |
| born in Malaysia although | マレーシア生まれですが |
| his father came from China. | お父さんは中国から来ました。 |
| He told me he was 68 and | 彼は68歳だと言い |
| he said he would take me | 私に |
| on a tour of the city | 市内観光をしてくれ |
| and tell me everything. | 色々教えてくれると言いました。 |
| "Everyone likes me. | 「皆が私を好きだよ。 |
| I tell you about Malacca. | マラッカのことを話してあげるよ。 |
| I was born here. | 生まれはここだよ。 |
| I remember the Japanese. | 日本人を覚えている。 |
| Are you French?" | あんたフランス人？」 |
| I gave Mr.Ong the brochure | 私はオングさんに例のパンフ |
| I was just given | レットを渡し |
| and told him to take me there. | そこに連れて行ってくれと言いました。 |
| | |
| As we went he kept talking, | 進みながら彼は話し続けました |
| his muscles straining | 筋肉をはちきらせんばかりに |
| to pedal me around | 私を乗せ自転車をこぎ |
| in the blistering sun | 灼熱の太陽の下でした |
| and I kept thinking, | 私はずっと考え続けていました |
| "This guy really works hard." | 「この人は本当によく働くな。」 |
| About 10 minutes later we arrived. | 約10分後に着きました。 |

## §4　通訳基本練習

### (1)　日英通訳練習

右ページの解答例にとらわれない自然な訳出を目指して下さい。

**食べ物**

1　私は好き嫌いがありません。
2　私は大食漢です。
3　私はグルメではありません。
4　私は天プラが好きです。
5　食欲がなくなった。
6　父は料理がうまい。
7　私はよく中華料理を食べます。
8　私は週に2，3度外食します。
9　ビールを飲むとじんま疹がでます。
10　果物の中で私が好きなのはみかんです。
11　あの子は甘い物が好きです。
12　飲み込む前によく嚙みます。
13　昨日飲み過ぎて胃がむかつく。
14　彼女は拒食症だ。
15　菜食主義の人達は玉子も食べないのですか。
16　オムレツとモヤシ炒めなら作れます。
17　このエスニック料理は食欲をそそる。
18　彼によると激辛カレーは体にいいそうだ。
19　ポークカツにはキャベツの千切りが添えてあります。
20　青柳さんは食中毒のため欠席です。

### (2)　ワン・センテンス遅れ通訳の練習

上記の1～20のワン・センテンス遅れ通訳を練習して下さい。特に長文は数回練習するのがよいでしょう。

英日通訳練習

日本語に即時変換して下さい。

## Food

1　I can eat anything.
2　I'm a big eater.
3　I'm not a gourmet.
4　I like Tempura.
5　I lost my appetite.
6　My father is a good cook.
7　I often have Chinese food.
8　I dine out a few times a week.
9　When I have beer, I get a rash.
10　Of fruits, I like tangerines the best.
11　The child has a sweet tooth.
12　I chew well before swallowing.
13　I drank too much yesterday and now my stomach is upset.
14　She is anorexic.
15　Don't vegetarians eat eggs?
16　I can make omelettes and fried bean sprouts.
17　This ethnic food is appetizing.
18　He says the hottest curry is good for his health.
19　Pork cutlet comes with shredded cabbage.
20　Mr. Aoyagi is absent because of food poisoning.

## §5　サイト・トランスレーションとリテイン処理

　視訳, サイトラとも呼ばれるサイト・トランスレーションの方法を確認して下さい。『頭ごなし訳』の手法を使用し, 実際の文章を口頭訳出していきます。この際, 目は先に読み進みます。口頭訳出のスピードに支障がない場合は, 文章を訳し上げてもかまいません。スピードが落ちる場合は文末からの訳し上げ和訳をしないことが肝心です。また, 場合によっては自然な日本語訳出のために, 訳語をリテイン（記憶保持）しておき, 適当なところで訳出することも必要です。

### リテイン処理の練習

　カッコでくくられた語句をリテインして文の最後で訳出します。

1　The Japanese Labor Standards Law　　日本の労働基準法は
　　〔has set〕working hours　　労働時間を
　　at 40 hours per week.　　週40時間と定めている。

2　In business,〔it is believed〕that an employee's ability increases with length of service.

3　The unions are usually〔formed〕on the basis of a company.

4　The Water Pollution Control Law〔is designed to〕prevent the pollution of water.

5　The aid program〔stresses〕assistance in job training, and energy development.

6　In 1854 the US and Japan〔concluded〕a treaty of amity.

### 解答例

リテイン練習
2　企業では従業員の勤続年数に従って能力が増すと考えられている。
3　組合は通常，会社単位で組織化されている。
4　水質汚染規制法は水の汚染を防止するのが目的です。
5　援助計画は職業訓練とエネルギー開発に力を入れている。
6　1854年にアメリカと日本は友好条約を結んだ。

**練習**　頭ごなしの訳出法を用い，サイトラ（視訳）して下さい。　🅟1-9

　I like Nikko. The nature there is really beautiful. There are mountains, valleys, forests and cascades. If you take the 9:00 express train you can get there before 11:00. The ride is nice and comfortable. You can enjoy the scenery on the way. You see a lot of farmhouses.
　I often think it would be nice to live on a farm.
　Sometimes I go hiking in summer. It's a nice feeling to be in a mountain forest.
　The air is clean and it's very peaceful. If I hike to the top of the mountain, I can get a good view of the surrounding areas. I feel the world is so big and I'm so small.
　This is a nice feeling.

### 解答例

サイトラ
　私は日光が好きです。そこの自然は本当に美しいです。山あり，谷あり，森も滝もあります。9時の特急に乗れば11時前に着けます。電車の旅は快適です。途中景色も楽しめます。農家がたくさん見えます。農園に住むのは楽しいのではないかとよく思います。
　夏には時々，ハイキングに行きます。山林の中は気持ちがいいです。空気は清浄で，静かです。山頂にハイキングすると，周辺の景色がみられます。世界をとても大きく感じ，私は本当に小さいと感じます。すごくいい気持ちです。

# Lesson 3

## §1 クイック・レスポンス

(1) ボキャビル

**演習方法**

日本語と英語の合成語を2秒以内で発音し意味を確認します。
次に日本語から英語，英語から日本語へ即時変換して下さい。

## Season, weather & Asia is close 3

| | | |
|---|---|---|
| 1 | 気象の | meteorological |
| 2 | 寒冷前線 | cold front |
| 3 | 天気予報 | weather forecast |
| 4 | 曇りの | overcast |
| 5 | 気圧 | pressure |
| 6 | 湿度 | humidity |
| 7 | 降水量 | precipitation |
| 8 | 薄曇りの | slightly (or partly) cloudy |
| 9 | 小雨 | drizzle |
| 10 | ひょう，あられ | hail |
| 11 | 吹く | blow |
| 12 | 雷 | thunder |
| 13 | 稲妻 | lightning |
| 14 | 凍る | freeze |
| 15 | しめっぽい | humid |
| 16 | そよ風 | breeze |
| 17 | どしゃぶり | downpour |
| 18 | 家系 | descent |
| 19 | 他の予定でふさがっている | I'm booked up |
| 20 | 来週の今日 | a week from today |

(2) **数字** 英語に変換して下さい。

1万，1万2千，3万5千，5万5千，4千5百，6万7千，
8千，9千，4千8百，3千7百，7千9百，9万9千，6千，
4万，3万6千，7万，5万4千，6万6千，6万6千5百

## §2 リテンションとリプロダクション

(1) **リテンション練習**
数回音読して暗唱して下さい。

A  I'll be coming on a short business trip to Kobe. So I'd like to visit you if it is OK.
B  That's fine with me. When do you think you can come?
A  Would a week from today be convenient for you?
B  I'm checking my schedule so please hold on. Oh, sorry, I'm booked up on that day. How about a week from Friday? I have nothing scheduled for the afternoon.
A  Then I'll come by your office after lunch.

(2) **リプロダクション**
日本語文を読み，または聞き，即時に訳出して下さい。

A  神戸に短期出張します。そこであなたを訪問したいと思っているのですがよろしいでしょうか。
B  いいですよ。いつお出でになれますか。
A  一週間後ではいかがですか。
B  スケジュールをチェックしてますからちょっと待ってて下さい。
   ああ，ごめんなさい。その日はもう予定が詰まっています。
   次の次の金曜日ではどうですか。その日の午後なら予定は何も入っていません。
A  では，昼食後オフィスにうかがいます。

## §3 区切り聞き

**演習方法**

初回の区切り聞きでリピーティング，二回目は該当部の日本語訳を音読して下さい。三回目から自分の言葉で通訳して下さい。

最後にシャドーイングをして達成度をチェックします。

## Asia is close 3

1-11

| | |
|---|---|
| Inside I met the manager, | 中で支配人に会いました |
| a friendly and polite young man | 親切な礼儀正しい若者で |
| of Indian descent named Iqbal, | インド系のイクバルという名の人で |
| who showed me the room. | 彼が部屋を見せてくれました。 |
| I asked him how much | 私は彼に聞きました |
| I should pay Mr. Ong. | オングさんにいくら払うべきかを |
| "Give him 3 ringgits. | 「3リンギットあげて下さい。 |
| We give him 2." | 我々が2リンギット払います。」 |
| Iqbal handed Mr. Ong 2 | イクバルは2リンギット渡し |
| ringgits and I handed him 3 | 私は彼に3リンギット手渡し |
| and then remembered | 思い出しました |
| how hard he worked | 彼が一生懸命働いたことを |
| and gave him 2 more. | それで2リンギット余計にあげました。 |
| I told Mr. Ong | 私はオングさんに言いました |
| I'd be staying at the lodge | 私はこのロッジに泊まり |
| and that I'd maybe take his tour | 彼の観光ツアーを後で利用するかも |
| later. | しれないと。 |
| Mr. Ong showed me a notebook | 彼はノートを見せてくれました。 |
| which his customers | 彼の客達が |
| had written in. | 書込みしたものです |
| "Mr. Ong is a nice guy. | 「オングさんはいい人だ。 |

| | |
|---|---|
| He gave us a very interesting | 彼は非常に面白い |
| tour of Malacca | マラッカ観光をさせてくれ |
| and told us things | 色々話してくれ |
| that we couldn't have learned | 教えてくれました |
| anywhere else. | 他では学べないようなことまで |
| Michael from New Zealand." | ニュージーランドからのマイケル。」 |
| Another read. | その他に書いてあるのは |
| "We had a wonderful time | 「私たちは素晴らしいひと時を |
| with Mr.Ong. | オングさんと過ごしました。 |
| He works hard | 彼は一生懸命働きます |
| even though he is 65. | 65歳という年齢なのに。 |
| Tina and Susan March 85." | ティナとスーザン85年3月。」 |
| I read this last one and thought | 最後の文を読んで思いました |
| this should make him 75 not 68 | と言うことは彼は75歳で |
| as he told me earlier. | さっき言った68ではないのだ。 |

| | |
|---|---|
| One night at the lodge | ある晩ロッジで |
| where I was staying | 私が宿泊していたところですが |
| Mr. and Mrs. Lee, the owners, | オーナーのリー夫妻が |
| arranged for the guests to eat | 取り計らい，ゲストが |
| at a Chinese restaurant in town. | 町の中華料理店に行きました |
| The food was delicious and | 食事は美味しく |
| fellow dinner companions were | 一緒にディナーを食べた人達も |
| interesting. | 面白い人達でした。 |
| At our table were Australians, | テーブルにはオーストラリア人 |
| a Frenchman, an Italian, | フランス人，イタリア人， |
| a Dutchman, a Dane | オランダ人，デンマーク人 |
| and me, the American. | それにアメリカ人の私 |
| A good group for international | インターナショナルな会話が |
| conversation. | 出来るいいグループでした。 |
| (written in 1995) | |

## §4 通訳基本練習

### (1) 日英通訳練習
#### 天候と季節

1　日本では四季がはっきりしています。
2　夏は暑くて湿度が高いです。
3　ところによっては雪がたくさん降ります。
4　春は4月初めごろからです。
5　強風注意報が出ていますから遊泳禁止です。
6　梅雨は6月初めから始まり2〜3週間続きます。
7　台風のためフェリーが欠航しました。
8　秋には美しい紅葉が見られます。
9　冬には2メートルも雪が積もることがあります。
10　彼は花粉症でこの時期にはマスクをつけて歩きます。
11　小春日和は気持ちがいい。
12　海に雷が落ちました。
13　夕立のあとに虹が出た。
14　毎年今頃の朝にはよく霧がかかります。
15　50年振りにいわゆる熱帯夜の記録が塗り替えられました。

### (2) ワン・センテンス遅れ通訳の練習
#### 東京の四季

東京では四季がはっきりしています。3月の終わりごろから4月の初めころに春がやってきます。桜の花が開花するのは3月第3週のころです。六月には梅雨があり、これが2週間ほど続きます。夏は暑くなります。湿度も高くあまり快適ではありません。秋はとても美しい季節です。9月ころになると木の葉が色づきます。そしてだんだん葉が落ち、気温も低くなっていきます。11月終りから12月始めになると一段と寒さが厳しくなります。

## Weather & Seasons  🔊 1-12

1. We have four distinct seasons in Japan.
2. It is hot and humid in summer.
3. We get a lot of snow in some areas.
4. Spring begins around early April.
5. As there's the strong wind alert, it is prohibited to swim.
6. The rainy season begins in early June and lasts for a few weeks.
7. The ferry service was canceled because of a typhoon.
8. We can enjoy beautiful fall colors in autumn.
9. Sometimes snow falls to a depth of 2 meters in the winter.
10. Because of hay fever he wears a mask at this time of year.
11. It feels good in Indian summer.
12. The thunderbolt fell in the sea.
13. A rainbow came out after a shower.
14. It gets misty in the morning at this time of year.
15. For the first time in 50 years the record of so called tropical nights was broken.

## The seasons of Tokyo  🔊 1-13

We have 4 distinct seasons in Tokyo. Spring comes at the end of March or at the beginning of April. The cherry blossoms start to bloom around the third week of March. In June we have a rainy season, and this lasts for about 2 weeks. It gets hot in summer. Humidity gets high and it's not so comfortable. In September leaves turn colors and it gets very beautiful. Then gradually the leaves fall, and the temperature gets lower. From around the end of November and at the beginning of December, it really becomes cold.

## §5 メモ取り練習

メモ取りとメモ用マーク例

1. 慣れるまではなるべく詳細にメモします。
2. 慣れたら名詞と数字を中心にメモを取り，要約通訳して下さい。
3. 主語は変わる時のみノートし，なるべく動詞もリテインします。
   リテイン事項（メモしない事項）を明確に決めておくとメモ取りの負担をやや軽減できます。例；動詞はリテインし→（矢印）で表します。
4. 頻出語と長い語はいつも同じマークにすると能率的です。
5. メモは文脈が再生できる記憶の補助ツールです。内容のイメージを瞬時に呼び起こすことができるフローチャートを作成するつもりで枝葉は切り捨てます。
6. メモは日本語で取っても英語でも，両方の混合でもいいのですが，リスニング試験の対策としては英語でのメモ取りが便利です。

メモ用マーク例を元に，頻出語のマークを工夫して下さい。

| | | | | | | |
|---|---|---|---|---|---|---|
| **Group 1** | 過去形 studied＝std' | | 進行形 going＝go" | | | |
| | 未来系 will | ＞＞ | do＝ | ヽ | will do＝ | ＞＞ヽ |
| | did | ヾ | know | kn | hand | ҹ |
| | like | lik | love | ♡ | thank | θx |
| | think | θ | understand | 了 | want | ☆ |
| | see | 👁 ⌒ | hear | ⤴ | speak | □, ⌣ |
| | look | 👁 ⌒ | listen | ⤴ | say | □, ⌣ |
| | watch | 👁 ⌒ | eat | □⌣ | tell | □, ⌣ |
| **Group 2** | time | T | then | ð | morning | m̊ |
| | year | yr | week | wk | afternoon | å |
| | office | ofc | store | 广 | evening | e̊ |
| | earth | ⊿ | world | ⊖ | intenational | ⊖l |
| **Group 3** | economy | 圣 | manager | mng人 | number | # ↓ |
| | new | nu | happy | ☺ | under | |

more　　　＜　　less　　＞　　until　　　→|

# メモ　ベーシック・スタイル

左上から右下に向けて主語，動詞，目的語と順次に一段ずつ下に書きます。

　　In the summer of 1959, something did go wrong with the power plant that provides New York with electricity.

　　　　59年夏　　　　　　　　　　　59年の夏
　　　　　　　　　　　　　　　　　　　　　ニューヨークに電力を供給する
　　　　　　発電　X　　　　　　　　　　　発電所で何かが故障しました。
　　　　　　　｜
　　　　　　　NY　☼
　　　　　　　　　　　　　　　＊この文章では文脈から発電所で何か
　　　　　　　　　　　　　　　　が故障したと推測できるので動詞句
　　　　　　　　　　　　　　　　は不要となります。
　　　　　　　　　　　　　　　＊関係代名詞の処理法を検討して下さ
　　　　　　　　　　　　　　　　い。


　　Apparently, we express our emotions and attitudes more nonverbally than verbally.

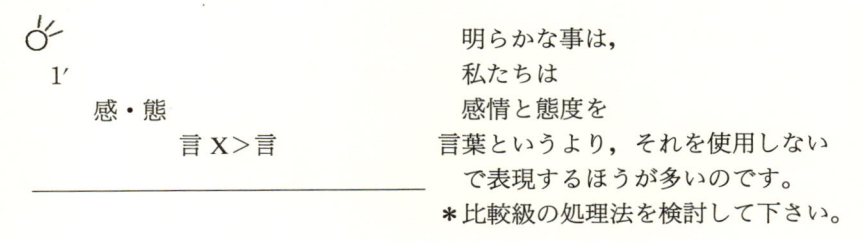

　　☼　　　　　　　　　　　　　　明らかな事は，
　　　1'　　　　　　　　　　　　　私たちは
　　　　感・態　　　　　　　　　　感情と態度を
　　　　　　言 X＞言　　　　　　　言葉というより，それを使用しない
　　　　　　　　　　　　　　　　　で表現するほうが多いのです。
　　　　　　　　　　　　　　　＊比較級の処理法を検討して下さい。

### メモ参考例  ♪1-14

I'd like you to meet Professor Bill Robinson, our new advisor. As all of you know his discovery enabled our company to provide consumers with more effective fertilizers for all types of plants.

In this seminar I would like Professor Robinson to share his ideas and on what he has planned for the future. I'm sure his words will be encouragement and inspiration to us. Now everybody, will you join me in welcoming Professor Robinson.

リスニング試験または逐次通訳用メモはできるだけ詳細に取ります。

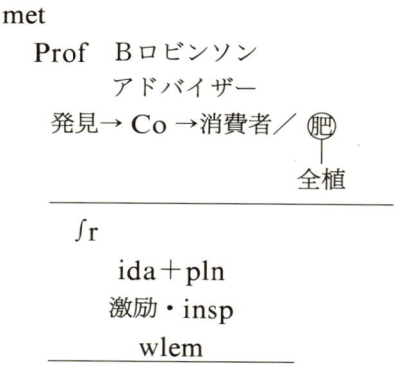

   met
  Prof Bロビンソン
     アドバイザー
  発見→ Co →消費者／㊥
      │
      全植
  ―――――――――――
   ∫r
   ida＋pln
   激励・insp
  ―――――――――――
    wlem

ウィスパリング同時通訳用メモは，最後に訳す動詞，絶対に間違えてはならない名詞や数字などを中心にノートします。

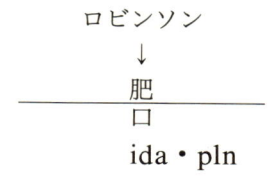

   ロビンソン
    ↓
 ――――――肥―――――――
    口
   ida・pln

## メモ取り練習　メモ化して下さい。　1-15

1　How large a (　　　　) is there in the plant?

2　I cannot (　　　　) any issues we need to discuss.

3　I want to examine those (　　　　).

4　We are having (　　　　) at the (　　　　) next month.

5　I think we have good (　　　　) and they should be (　　　　).

6　(　　　　) no (　　　　) since we opened 9 years ago.

7　I want to ask a few questions about (　　　　).

8　Our (　　　　) are going (　　　　) the roof.

9　It is better to (　　　) a copy of new (　　　　).

10　(　　　　) a way to cut (　　　　).

### 解答

1　work force
2　think of
3　allocations
4　an exhibit, trade fair
5　products, in demand
6　We've had, serious accidents
7　capital expenditure
8　shipping costs, through
9　attach, apecifications
10　We've got to find, expenses

# Lesson 4

## §1 クイック・レスポンス

(1) ボキャビル

**演習方法**

日本語と英語の合成語を2秒以内で発音して意味を確認します。次に日本語から英語，英語から日本語へ即時変換して下さい。

### Travel & Asia is close 2

| | | |
|---|---|---|
| 1 | 一人旅する | travel by oneself |
| 2 | 清算する | adjust |
| 3 | 乗り換え | transfer |
| 4 | 確認する | confirm |
| 5 | お土産 | souvenir |
| 6 | 山荘 | summer house |
| 7 | 民宿 | tourist home |
| 8 | ペンション | rental cottage |
| 9 | 旅程 | itinerary |
| 10 | 非常口 | emergency exit |
| 11 | 寺 | temple |
| 12 | 神社 | Shinto shrine |
| 13 | 五重の塔 | 5-storied pagoda |
| 14 | 鳥居 | Torii gate |
| 15 | 宿泊施設 | accommodations |
| 16 | 満室 | No vacancy |
| 17 | 〜に関しては | as for |
| 18 | 〜するつもり | intend(ing) to |
| 19 | しがみついた，執着する | cling(ing) to |
| 20 | 持ち主 | proprietor |

(2) **数字**　英語に変換して下さい。

1万5千，6万8千，8万5百，4万7百，10万1千，50万，
12万，51万，62万，62万3千，1万9千5百，9万6千，9万，
22万6千，8万7千，17万，5万，30万5千，2万3千7百，30万，
14万5百，49万，51万5千，12万5千，15万，19万6千，80万

## §2　リテンションとリプロダクション

### (1)　リテンション練習
数回音読して暗唱して下さい。　　　　　　　　　1-16

A　The details of the contract leave much to be desired on our part.
B　What do you mean?
A　I don't think we should go ahead and sign it yet.
B　What's bothering you?
A　I think some of the articles have to be changed.
B　Well, could you clarify them for me?

### (2)　リプロダクション
日本語文を読み，または聞き，即時に訳出して下さい。

A　契約の細部はこちら側からはまだまだ不満です。
B　どういうことですか？
A　このまま進めていってサインをするべきではないと思います。
B　何が気になっているのですか？
A　条項の幾つかは変えなければならないと思います。
B　明確に言って下さいますか？

## §3　区切り聞き

**演習方法**

初回の区切り聞きでリピーティング，二回目は該当部の日本語訳を音読して下さい。三回目から自分の言葉で通訳して下さい。

## Asia is close 4　　🎧 1-17

| | |
|---|---|
| One more person that will stay in my memory for a while | もう一人 しばらく記憶に残る人は |
| is a taxi driver of | タクシーの運転手 |
| Indian descent named Velu. | インド系のベルです。 |
| I got into his taxi | 彼のタクシーに乗ったのは |
| about 6 o'clock one evening | 夕方の6時頃で |
| intending to go back to the lodge. | ロッジに帰るつもりでした。 |
| "I will take you on a tour. | 「見物ツアーはどうですか |
| 20 Ringgit one hour." | 一時間20リンギットですが。」 |
| I said OK and in that next hour | 私はOKし次の時間に |
| we became great friends. | 私たちはよい友達になったのです。 |
| He gave me his address | 彼は私に住所と |
| and phone number, | 電話番号をくれ |
| invited me to lunch | 昼食に招いてくれました |
| at his home the next day, | 自宅に翌日きてくれと，そして |
| and gave me a great tour of Malacca. | 素晴らしいマラッカ見物をさせてくれました。 |
| One very interesting place was | 非常に面白かったのは |
| what Velu called a Portuguese | ベルがポルトガル人町と呼んだ |
| town along Jalan, (meaning road), | ジャラン，道という意味ですが |
| D'Albuquerque. | ダルバカーキ通りです。 |
| In this section of town, | この地域には |
| people of Portuguese descent | ポルトガル系の人々が |

| | |
|---|---|
| still live, clinging to | いまだに住んでいて |
| their culture in some ways. | その文化に何らかの形でしがみついているのです。 |
| | |
| As we got out of the taxi | タクシーを降りていると |
| a proprietor came up to me | ある企業経営者がやって来て |
| and asked if I wanted a beer. | ビールをどうかと尋ねました。 |
| He looked European, | 彼はヨーロッパ人に見えました。 |
| not Asian. | アジア人には見えませんでした。 |
| It was shocking to realize | ショックだったのは |
| that here was a man living | ここにこの人が住んでいること |
| in a very small community | 小さいコミュニティの中で |
| descended from Portuguese settlers who had come to this area | ポルトガルの移住者の子孫として先祖がここに |
| 400 years ago and had somehow | 400年前にやって来て，何とか |
| retained their community. | コミュニティが残っていること |
| Truly amazing. | 本当に驚くべきことです。 |
| A small Portuguese community | 小さいポルトガルのコミュニティ |
| where the world has passed by. | ここでは世界が通り過ぎてきたのです。 |
| | |
| As I said earlier one thing | 前にもいったように一つ |
| I like about Japan | 日本で気にいっているのは |
| is that the rest of Asia | アジアの他の国々が |
| is not so far away. | そんなに遠くないことです。 |
| Mr. Ong is a good example of | オングさんは良い例です |
| what makes traveling great. | 旅行を素晴らしいものにする |
| People. | 人間です。 |
| The sites are interesting, | 場所は興味深く |
| the food can be delicious | 食べ物は美味しい |
| but the people are what stay | でも，人々が |
| in your mind. | 心に残るのです。 |

## §4　通訳基本練習

### (1)　日英通訳練習
### 旅行と自然

1　外国にいったことありますか。
2　パッケージ・ツアーは便利ですよ。
3　富士山の五合目まではバスで行けます。
4　新幹線は15分ごとに走っています。
5　来月は奈良の大仏を見に行くつもりです。
6　正月休みには温泉に行きたい。
7　竜安寺の石庭はぜひ見なければならない所です。
8　私はドイツに2度行ったことがあります。
9　ロンドンまでの飛行時間はどのくらいですか。
10　宇宙にはたくさんの銀河がある。
11　熱帯雨林が消えてゆく。
12　タイタニック号は氷山にぶつかった。
13　酸性雨に対して措置を講じなければなりません。
14　あの山が噴火したのは1707年です。
15　私の趣味はハイキングとバード・ウォッチングです。
16　オリエント急行で旅をしたいと思っています。

### (2)　ワン・センテンス遅れ通訳の練習
### 旅行について

　もし日本に旅行なさるつもりでしたら冬がいいですよ。この時期には旅行客が少ないですから，観光地が静かでいいのですよ。冬は，雨は余り降りません。

　旅館に泊まるのも面白い経験です。旅館とは日本式のインです。宿泊料金には朝食とディナーが含まれています。多くの旅館には露天風呂があります。露天風呂に入って自然の美しさを楽しむのは素晴らしいですよ。

## Travel and Nature  1-18

1. Have you been abroad?
2. Package tours are convenient.
3. You can get to the 5th stage of Mt. Fuji by bus.
4. The "Bullet trains" run every 15 minutes.
5. I plan to go to Nara to see the Great Buddha next month.
6. I want to go to a hot spring during the New Year holidays.
7. The stone garden of Ryoanji is a must.
8. I've been to Germany twice.
9. How long is the flight time to London?
10. There are a lot of galaxies in the Universe.
11. The tropical rain forest is disappearing.
12. The Titanic crashed into an iceburg.
13. We must take measures against acid rain.
14. That mountain erupted in 1707.
15. My hobbies are hiking and bird watching.
16. I want to travel by the Orient Express.

## Travel  1-19

If you want to travel to Japan, do it in winter. In this season we have fewer tourists, so it is nice and quiet in sightseeing places. It doesn't rain so much in winter.

Staying in a Ryokan is also an interesting experience. A ryokan is a Japanese-style inn. Japanese breakfast and dinner are included in the room charge. Many inns have outdoor baths. It's wonderful to take a bath enjoying the beauty of nature at the same time.

# §5　商談通訳

英語は日本語に日本語は英語に通訳して下さい。
一応の流れがつかめたらウィスパリング同時通訳で練習します。
（CDには英文のみが録音されています。）

## 接待　1　乾杯　　　1-20

Dr. Wagner, Vice president　Sociedad Anonima de Tintura
Ms. Yokota, President　　　Japan Chemical Dye
At a restaurant afrer signing contract for partnership

**Yokota:** 契約が締結されたことを祝って懐石料理にしました。
懐石は非常に特別なものなのです。
でもまず初めに，事業の成功を祝って乾杯しましょう。

**Wagner and Yokota:**　Kampai.

**Wagner:** Well, I'd like to thank you for your efforts to finalize the deal. I'm very honored to be able to do business with you as a partner.

**Yokota:** 目標に到達するには長い道程がありますが，信頼できるパートナーをもてましたから，きっと目標に到達できると確信しています。そして，はるばるパナマからおこし頂いて感謝しております。

**Wagner:** Not at all. I'm very happy that I could come here and make new friends.

**Yokota:** では，料理を楽しんでいただければと願っています。

## 接待　1　　Raising a Toast

Dr. ワーグナー　　副社長　　ティンテューラ株式会社
Ms. 横田　　　　社長　　　日本化学染料
パートナー契約を締結した後レストランで

**Yokota:** To celebrate signing the contract, we are having Kaiseki, which is very special to us. But first of all, let us drink to a successful business relationship.

**Wagner and Yokota:** 乾杯。

**Wagner:** さて，この取引をまとめるためのご尽力にたいしてお礼を申し上げます。
パートナーとしてご一緒に事業が出来るのは光栄です。

**Yokota:** We'll have to go a long way to achieve our goal, but having a reliable partner, we are sure to achieve what we aim at. And I appreciate your coming all the way from Panama.

**Wagner:** どう致しまして。こちらに来て新しい友人を得られて嬉しく思っています。

**Yokota:** Well, I hope you enjoy the food.

# Lesson 5

## §1 クイック・レスポンス

(1) ボキャビル

**演習方法**

　　日本語と英語の合成語を2秒以内で発音して意味を確認します。
次に日本語から英語，英語から日本語へ即時変換して下さい。

## Travel & Eating for International Understanding 1

| | | |
|---|---|---|
| 1 | 神を信じる | believe in God |
| 2 | 洗礼 | baptism |
| 3 | 祈る | pray |
| 4 | 僧 | priest |
| 5 | 宣教師 | missionary |
| 6 | 信奉者 | adherent |
| 7 | 人格化 | personification |
| 8 | 教義 | doctrine |
| 9 | 埋める，埋葬する | bury |
| 10 | 現象 | phenomena |
| 11 | 信仰 | faith |
| 12 | 捧げ物 | offering |
| 13 | 救われる | be saved |
| 14 | 生れ変わる | reincarnate |
| 15 | 掘り下げる | dig into |
| 16 | エキゾチックな食べ物 | exotic delicacy |
| 17 | 義務的に | dutifully |
| 18 | 儀式 | rite |
| 19 | 話が脱線する | digress |
| 20 | 充分な証拠 | ample evidence |

(2) **数字**　英語に変換して下さい。

1914年，1923年，1964年，1945年，1603年，794年
1192年，710年，1333年，1590年，1868年，1467年

## §2　リテンションとリプロダクション

(1) **リテンション練習**
数回音読して暗唱して下さい。　　　　　　　　　🅒 1-21

A　Are you, Mr. Winkel, in charge of the Purchasing Department?
B　No. I'm his assistant. Mr. Winkel is in a meeting now.
A　Oh, I see. I'm here to meet him to give him our new catalog. I'm Ozaki from Kanda International.
　 I'd appreciate it if you could consider our new products for the future.
B　You know we have a number of suppliers.
A　I believe our products will save you time and money.

(2) **リプロダクション**
日本語文を読み，または聞いて，即時に訳出して下さい。

A　ウィンクルさんですか購買部担当の？
B　いいえ，私はアシスタントです。ウィンクルはただ今会議中です。
A　ああそうですか。私どもの新しいカタログを差し上げようと参りました。私神田インターナショナルの尾崎と申します。
　 将来的に私どもの製品をご考慮いただければ有り難いのですが。
B　ご存じのように私どもには納入業者が何軒もあります。
A　私どもの製品で時間とコストを節約できると存じます。

## §3 区切り聞き

**演習方法**

初回の区切り聞きでリピーティング，二回目は該当部の日本語訳を音読して下さい。三回目から自分の言葉で通訳して下さい。

# Eating For International Understanding 1 🄫 1-22
### Greg O'Dowd

| | |
|---|---|
| When I first came to Japan, | 初めて日本に来たとき |
| I was very surprised by | 驚いたのは |
| the number of television | テレビで |
| programs concerning food | 食べ物関係 |
| and international cuisine | と外国料理の |
| in particular. | 番組が多いことでした。 |
| It seemed that | どうやら |
| at almost any time | |
| of the day or night | 年がら年中 |
| you could turn on the television | テレビをつけると |
| and find a program | やっていて |
| about *ramen, sushi, gyoza,* | ラーメン，すし，餃子， |
| Chinese food or others, | 中華料理やその他 |
| all cooked by professional chefs | プロが作ったものを |
| and tasted by several "talents". | タレント達が賞味するものです。 |
| They would then | それから |
| dutifully follow this rite | 義務的に |
| with "oishiiiiii" or "umai!!" | 『美味しい』とか『旨い』 |
| It seemed that | と言うのです |
| everything they ate | 食べた物が全て |
| was ultra delicious. | 非常においしくみえます。 |
| Well, I suppose | まあ， |
| not many sponsors | スポンサーは |

| | |
|---|---|
| would want to have their products associated with a program where specially invited "talents" | いやでしょう。自社製品が関係している番組でゲストのタレントが |
| sampled some exotic delicacy and then with a grimace spat it on the floor at the time of consumption. | エキゾチックな食べ物を味わって嫌な顔をして床にそれを吐きだしたりしたら食べた途端に。 |
| Anyway, I digress. | とにかく, 余談ですが |
| There appears to be ample evidence to suggest | 充分証拠が挙げられます。 |
| that Japanese people | 日本人は |
| have a special fascination | 特別 |
| with foreign cuisine. | 外国料理が好きなようです。 |
| This is indeed | 本当に |
| a very healthy development | 健全な発展ぶりと言えましょう。 |
| in a country which has professed it is making all out efforts | 努力して |
| to "internationalize" itself. | 国際化を目指している国として。 |
| What better way to come to understand | 他にもっと良い方法はあるでしょうか |
| other cultures | 他国の文化を理解するのは |
| than by digging into their national food. | その国の食物を良く知ることです。 |
| Just the thing to break down national barriers | まさにこれが国の障壁を打破るもので |
| and bring people closer together. | 人々を親密にさせるものです。 |
| Mind you, it might not all be steak and cake. | いいですか。それは全てがステーキやケーキとは限りません。 |

## §4 商談通訳

日本語は英語，英語は日本語へ通訳して下さい。
(CDには英文のみが録音されています。)

### 接待　2　茶道について　1-23

(Ms. Ford and Ms. Takano are in the Japanese garden lounge of a hotel.)

Ford: I understand the tea ceremony is one of Japan's traditional arts. Where do you grow your tea?

Takano: 多くは静岡で栽培されています，富士山の近くです。

Ford: Speaking of tea, could you please tell me a little about the tea ceremony itself?

Takano: お茶は仏教徒により中国から日本にもたらされました。そして茶道は16世紀に僧の千の利休により確立されました。彼によると茶室は"静寂"のある場所です。そこは人が自然と和合し黙想しようとする所です。

Ford: That sounds very nice.

Takano: 茶道で一番重要なモットーは一期一会です。一期とは人生，一会とは機会が一回という意味です。お茶をなさる時には，このお茶のお点前(てまえ)が人生で最初で最後だと思うのです。ですからお客様に最大の注意を払って差し上げるのです。また，無言のコミュニケーションが非常に大事だとされています。

Ford: It sounds very difficult.

Takano: それ程ではありません。一番大切なのは一期一会の精神です。それは禅の影響を受けていて，心の安らぎを得る助けになるのです。もしご興味をお持ちでしたら，お茶席にご案内しましょう。

## 接待 2　About Tea Ceremony

(Ms. フォードと Ms. 高野はホテルのガーデン・ラウンジにいます)

Ford: 茶道は日本の伝統芸能の一つですよね。お茶はどこで栽培されているのですか。

Takano: Most of it is grown in Shizuoka, near Mt. Fuji.

Ford: お茶といえば、茶道について少し教えて下さいますか。

Takano: Tea was introduced to Japan from China by Buddhists. And the "tea ceremony" was established by a monk named Sen no Rikyu in the 16th century. According to him, the tea room is where "tranquility" can be found. That's where one tries to harmonize oneself with nature and meditate.

Ford: それは素敵ですね。

Takano: In the tea ceremony, the most important motto is "Ichigo Iche." Ichigo means one's life, Ichie means one chance. When one does a tea ceremony, one thinks that the ceremony one performs is the first and last one in one's life. Therefore one tries to give one's utmost attention to guests. And communication without words is regarded very important.

Ford: 難しいですね。

Takano: Not really. The most important thing is the spirit of Ichigo-Ichie. It's influenced by Zen Buddhism and it helps achieve peace of mind.
If you're interested, we'll take you to a tea ceremony.

## §5 ディクテーション　　　　　　　🔊 1-24

CDを聞きながら空所に適語を書き入れて下さい。

1. Dr Hansen presents a very (　　) case for (　　　　)
   our (　　) quality control system.

2. I wonder why a staff meeting has been (　　) (　　) such
   a short (　　).

3. This (　　　) isn't quite ready. I think it (　　) use more
   (　　) in some sections.

4. We've placed advertisements about our new (　　) in the
   trade (　　　　). Also we scheduled many TV and
   radio (　　), too.

5. Here we (　　) many special safety (　　) because we
   keep (　　) of (　　　) dangerous chemicals.

6. It's a good idea that our (　　　) is considering (　　　　)
   abroad.

7. I had a chance to (　　　) the proposed budget for (　) next
   (　) year.

8. (　　) Ms. Debby Walenko, (　　) Ms. Debby Walenko of
   the New National Oil Company please come to the reception desk, you have an (　　) telephone call.

9. Mr Saito will speak to (　) today about (　　　　)
   (　　) (　　) foreign trade.

| ディクテーション | 解答 |

メモ化してください。

1. Dr Hansen presents a very positive case for restructuring our total quality control system.

2. I wonder why a staff meeting has been called on such a short notice.

3. This proposal isn't quite ready. I think it could use more details in some sections.

4. We've placed advertisements about our new line in the trade journals. Also we scheduled many TV and radio spots, too.

5. Here we employ many spcial safety measures because we keep dozens of potentially dangerous chemicals.

6. It's a good idea that our Board is considering marketing abroad.

7. I had a chance to review the proposed budget for the next fiscal year.

8. Paging Ms. Debby Walenko, would Ms. Debby Walenko of the New National Oil Company please come to the reception desk, you have an urgent telephone call.

9. Mr Saito will speak to us today about contemporary patterns in foreign trade.

# Lesson 6

## §1 クイック・レスポンス

(1) ボキャビル

**演習方法**

日本語と英語の合成語を2秒以内で発音します。
次に日本語から英語,英語から日本語へ即時変換して下さい。

## Art & Eating for International Understanding　2

| | | |
|---|---|---|
| 1 | 音楽家 | musician |
| 2 | 芸術家 | artist |
| 3 | 曲 | tune |
| 4 | 作曲する | compose |
| 5 | 拍手喝采する | applaud |
| 6 | ソリスト | soloist |
| 7 | デュエット | duet |
| 8 | トリオ | trio |
| 9 | 繰り返し | refrain |
| 10 | 歌詞 | verse |
| 11 | 指揮者 | conductor |
| 12 | 室内楽 | chamber music |
| 13 | 吸う | suck(ing) |
| 14 | 嘔吐袋 | barf bag |
| 15 | 影響する | affect |
| 16 | 吐きだす | exhale |
| 17 | しかし | nevertheless |
| 18 | 直感,洞察 | perception |
| 19 | 固い | rigid |
| 20 | 展示会 | exhibition |

(2) **数字**　英語に変換して下さい。

例　0.5（zero point five），　$\frac{2}{3}$（two thirds）
　　23.55，　　53.5，　　0.03，　　1/5，　　2/100，　　1/1000

## §2　リテンションとリプロダクション

### (1)　リテンション練習
数回音読して暗唱して下さい。　　　　　　　　🄯1-25

A　Thank you very much for coming to our exhibition today.
B　It looks fantastic. I'm going to take a good look at your displays.
A　Is there anything in particular that interests you?
　　If you would like to try out the new products on display I'd be happy to show you.
B　I'm interested in seeing that exhibit in Booth C.
A　I'm sorry that exhibit has been closed temporarily.
　　The attendant has just gone out for lunch. Please wait.
　　I'll try to find someone who can show it to you.

### (2)　リプロダクション
日本語文を読み，または聞き，即時に訳出して下さい。

A　本日，展示会におこし下さって誠にありがとうございます。
B　素晴らしいですね。ディスプレーを念を入れて見せて頂きます。
A　何か特にご興味がおありですか？もし展示の新製品を実際に試されたい場合は，ご遠慮なくおっしゃって下さい。
B　Cブースの展示に興味があります。
A　申し訳ございませんが，そちらは一時クローズされております。
　　係の者が食事にでておりますので，少々お待ち下さい。
　　それをお見せ出来る他の者を探してみましょう。

## §3 区切り聞き

**演習方法**

初回の区切り聞きでリピーティング，二回目は該当部の日本語訳を音読して下さい。三回目からは自分の言葉で通訳して下さい。

# Eating for International Understanding 2  1-26

| | |
|---|---|
| Just this morning, | 今朝 |
| when I turned on the TV, | テレビをつけると |
| I found a travel program | 旅行番組をやっていて |
| and, as I started to shovel | |
| the first spoonful of cornflakes | コーンフレークを食べながら |
| into my mouth, | 見ていると |
| saw a woman | 女の人が |
| dressed in colorful national dress sucking the eyes out of a sheep's head! | 民族衣装で羊の目をしゃぶり取ったのが映ったのです。 |
| Fortunately, the head wasn't still attached to the sheep; | 幸いにも羊の頭は胴体についていませんでした |
| nevertheless it did take me somewhat by surprise, | でも，ちょっと驚きました |
| causing me to exhale | それで |
| most of the cereal | シリアルを |
| onto the picture tube. | テレビに吹出してしまったのです。 |
| On the other hand, | しかし |
| I did learn something | 学びました |
| about another culture, | 他の文化を |
| basically, that if I ever go there | 基本的にそこに行くのだったら |
| I should take plenty of *cup ramen*. | カップ・ラーメンを持って行くべきだと。 |
| Oops, not a very | おっと，あまり |

| | |
|---|---|
| "international" conclusion! | 国際的な結論ではないですね。 |
| Anyway, I digress (again). | とにかく，話が脱線します。 |
| To get more to the point, | 要点を言いいます。 |
| it made me think more | 考えさせられたのは |
| about how eating can affect | 食することの影響で |
| our perceptions of other countries. | 国々についての印象が変わるということです。 |
| It's especially interesting | 特に面白いのは |
| to think that many dishes are | 多くの料理は |
| based on common ingredients, | ありふれた材料ででき， |
| for example, vegetables, meat, | 例えば野菜，肉， |
| sea food, salt, flour, eggs | 海産物，塩，小麦粉，卵 |
| and rice. | それに米です。 |
| In fact, | 事実 |
| rice is an interesting example. | 米は興味深い一例です。 |
| Rice is a very international food. | 米は非常に国際的な食物です。 |
| Many countries have national | 多くの国々には |
| dishes based on rice ; | 米をベースにした料理があります。 |
| fried rice in China, | 中国のチャーハン |
| Spanish paella, | スペインのパエリヤ |
| rice pudding in the U. K. | イギリスのライス・プディング |
| Australia's rice salad, | オーストラリアのライス・サラダ |
| and in the U. S. A. rice crispies. | そして米国のライス・クリスピー。 |
| However, not everyone | しかし |
| is so open-minded | 誰もが寛大であるとは限りません |
| when it comes to | つまり |
| eating their common food prepared in a slightly different way. | 自分達の食べ物をちょっと違った風に食べることに関しては。 |

## §4　商談通訳

日本語は英語，英語は日本語に通訳して下さい。

### 接待　3　能と歌舞伎　1-27

(Ms. Takano brings Ms. Ford back to her hotel by taxi.)

Ford: Speaking of Japanese arts, I have seen Kabuki in the States. I'm under the impression that Japanese traditional arts are very stylized and they emphasize refinement. This time I plan to see a Noh play. Unfortunately, I didn't have time to study it. What is it like?

Takano: 日本の芸術について本当に良く知っておられますね。
能は15世紀に世阿弥という名人により完成されました。
能で役者は面をつけ謡い舞います。でも動きはゆっくりしています。舞台は非常にユニークで背景には松が一本描かれてあるだけです。ですから想像力をはたらかせて情景を見ます。能のキーワードは幽玄です。つまり「静かで奥深さを持つ美」の意味です。

Ford: That's interesting. It means Noh is very different from Kabuki. I think Kabuki is more colorful.

Takano: その通りです。歌舞伎が女性により始められたのを知っておられましたか。現在は男の役者だけしかおりませんが。歌舞伎は17世紀に発展しました。能と比べると歌舞伎のほうが対話も動きも多く，わかりやすいのです。

Ford: I wish I had more time here to see Kabuki. Well, it's been a pleasant and informative night. And thanks to your kind attention.

Takano: お骨折りをいただきありがとうございました。おやすみなさい。

## 接待　3　Noh and Kabuki

(Ms. 高野は Ms. フォードをタクシーでホテルまで送ります。)

**Ford :** 日本の芸能についていえば，私はアメリカで歌舞伎を観たことがあります。私の印象では日本の伝統芸能は非常に様式化され，しかも洗練させる努力をしているように感じました。今回は能を観る予定です。残念なのですが，能について勉強する時間がありませんでした。能とはどの様なものなのですか。

**Takano :** You know quite a lot about our art. Noh was perfected by a master named Zeami in the 15th century. In Noh, the performers wear masks and chant and dance. But their movements are very slow. The stage is quite unique with only one pine tree painted on the backdrop. So you use your imagination to see the scenery. The key word for Noh is Yugen meaning "serene and profound beauty."

**Ford :** それは面白いですね。というと能は歌舞伎とはだいぶ違っているのですね。歌舞伎のほうが色彩が豊かだと思います。

**Takano :** That's right. Do you know that Kabuki was started by a woman although there are only actors now? Kabuki developed around the 17th century. Compared with Noh, Kabuki has more dialogues and actions, and it's easier to understand.

**Ford :** 歌舞伎が観賞出来る時間がもっとあったらいいのに。
さてと，今晩は楽しい有益な晩でした。お心遣いをありがとうございました。

**Takano :** I appreciate your efforts. Good night.

## §5 ディクテーション

まず全センテンスを頭ごなし翻訳，またはサイトラし，次に全文を聞いてメモを取り，要約通訳して下さい。時間制限1問につき5分　1-28

1  Good afternoon. Welcome to the World Trade Center. A _____ following _____ by our _____ Mr. Nagasaki. You may _____ and pick up your _____ there.

2  Now, I would like to introduce Mr. Valentine, _____ _____.
_____, Mr. Valentine was a professor of _____. He has spent _____ _____ in Hong Kong and Maccao.

3  I'd like you to meet Cynthia Moreno, _____.
Cynthia used to teach _____ in Spain. _____ she will be a _____ _____ our design department.

4  I _____ Professor Robinson. Prof. Robinson _____
_____ bio-chemistry. His discovery has _____ bio-chemical industry.
Immediately following _____ Prof. Robinson will _____.

まず全センテンスを頭ごなし翻訳，またはサイトラし，次に全文を聞いてメモを取り，要約通訳して下さい。

1 Good afternoon. Welcome to the World Trade Center. A guided tour of our facilities will begin promptly at 1:40 following an address by our chief executive officer Mr. Nagasaki. You may register in the auditorium and pick up your tour ID badge there.

2 Now, I would like to introduce Mr. Valentine, vice president and a member of the Board of directors.
Prior to joining our firm in 1991, Mr. Valentine was a professor of business administration. He has spent several years at our branch offices in Hong Kong and Maccao.

3 I'd like you to meet Cynthia Moreno, our new staff member. Cynthia used to teach at one of the best computer schools in Spain. With her extensive experience she will be a valuable addition to our design department.

4 I am pleased to introduce Professor Robinson. Prof. Robinson is known to many in our audience for his outstanding work in bio-chemistry. His discovery has revolutionized the bio-chemical industry.
Immediately following his presentation Prof. Robinson will take questions.

# Lesson 7

## §1 クイック・レスポンス

(1) ボキャビル

**演習方法**
日本語と英語の合成語を2秒以内で発音します。
次に日本語から英語，英語から日本語へ即時変換して下さい。

## Olympics & Eating for International Understanding

| | | |
|---|---|---|
| 1 | 勝つ | win |
| 2 | 負ける | lose |
| 3 | 引きわける | draw |
| 4 | 選手 | athlete |
| 5 | 延長戦 | overtime game |
| 6 | 応援する | cheer |
| 7 | 挑戦する | challenge |
| 8 | 新体操 | new gymnastics |
| 9 | 記録を破る | break the record |
| 10 | オリンピック | Olympic Games |
| 11 | 聖火リレー | sacred torch relay |
| 12 | 重量挙げ | weight lifting |
| 13 | 開催都市 | host city |
| 14 | 融通のきく | versatile |
| 15 | 全く | utter |
| 16 | 脅かす | threatening |
| 17 | 酢 | vinegar |
| 18 | 湯気がでる | steaming |
| 19 | 振りまく | sprinkle |
| 20 | 非難する | condemn(ing) |

(2) **数字** 日本語に即時変換して下さい。

Gate 6,　　Track 7,　　Chapter 1,　　Volume 8,　　Article 2,
the 18 th century,　　World War Two,　　Queen Elizabeth I

## §2　リテンションとリプロダクション

(1) **リテンション練習**
数回音読して暗唱して下さい。　　　　　　　　🅒 1-29

A　Has this product been marketed?
B　This product is available in Japan and in America, but we have no plans to market it in Europe.
A　Then could we buy that model over there?
B　I'm afraid I can't help you with your request.
　That is a display item and not for sale. But just in case, let me talk to the person in charge of sales.
　He may be able to answer your questions. Just a moment. I'll have him come right over.

(2) **リプロダクション**
日本語文を読み，または聞き，英語に即時に訳出して下さい。

A　製品は市場に出ていますか？
B　日本とアメリカでは手に入りますがヨーロッパで販売の予定はありません。
A　ではあそこのモデルを購入出来ますか。
B　申し訳ございませんがそのお申出にはそいかねます。
　あれは展示用品で非売品です。ですが，万が一ということもありますからセールス担当の者に話してみます。
　彼ならあなたのご質問にお答え出来るかもしれません。
　少々お待ち下さい。ただ今こちらに呼びます。

## §3 区切り聞き

**演習方法**

初回は区切り聞きでリピーティング，二回目は該当部の日本語訳を音読して下さい。三回目から自分の言葉で通訳して下さい。

# Eating for International Understanding 3  1-30

| | |
|---|---|
| Rice is a very versatile food. | 米は非常に多目的に使える食物です。 |
| Even in Japan, rice is used in a great variety of ways from *amazake* to *sushi*. | 日本においてでさえ米は色々な用いられ方をされます。甘酒から鮨まで色々です。 |
| However, it seems that versatility has its limits. | しかし，多様性にも限度があるようです。 |
| Even though in Japan rice is eaten as sweets | 日本で米はお菓子にして食べられますが， |
| some foreign variations often cause Japanese to have looks of utter disbelief overseas. What's wrong? | 外国での調理法を日本人に話すとよく信じられないという顔をされます。何がいけないのでしょうか？ |
| In Australia, many sweet rice products can be found rice custard, creamed rice and rice pudding. | オーストラリアでは甘い米製品が沢山あります。ライス・カスタード，クリーム・ライス，やライス・プディング。 |
| And in the summer barbecue season, what's wrong with making a delicious cold salad of rice with mayonnaise, vinegar, corn, peas and ham? | 夏のバーベキュー・シーズンにはいけませんか美味しく冷たいライス・サラダはマヨネーズ，酢，コーン，豆にハムを使います。 |
| It goes very well with a steak and a cold glass of beer. | ステーキにとてもよくあうのですそれから冷たいビールにも。 |

However, when I've explained this to my Japanese students their reaction couldn't be described as very "international." It's not a "bad" way to eat rice, it's just different!! However, I find the greatest reaction is to the simple story of eating rice in my childhood.
I can remember the excitement of my mother placing in front of me a big bowl of steaming boiled rice.
Then, a heavy sprinkling of sugar over the entire bowl followed by a flooding of cold milk-ummmm, oishiiiiii!
However my students' reaction is usually—aggh usooo, gero!!!
Yes, not very internationally-minded.
I always suggest
that they give it a try
before condemning it.
I tell them
that it may even make them feel more "international".
So far, no one has given me any feedback
on my suggestion.

でも、これを
日本の学生達に説明すると
彼等の反応はあまり
国際的とは言えませんでした。
米のまずい食べ方ではなく
違っているというだけなのに
でも一番大きい反応があったのは
単純な話でライスの食べ方でした
私の子供の頃の。
興奮したのを覚えています
母が
私の前に湯気が立った作りたての
御飯を
置き
砂糖を沢山ふりかけたのです
次に、冷たい
牛乳です。ウーン美味しーい。
しかし私の生徒達の反応は
普通ヤーだ、うっそー、げろ！
です。あまり
国際的な精神ではありません。
私がいつも言うのは
試してごらん
それから駄目だときめなさい。
私が言っているのは
それで彼等が
もっと国際的になれるかもしれないということです。今のところ
誰もフィード・バックをくれてません、私の提案したことに対して。

## §4 通訳基本練習

### (1) 日英通訳練習

## スポーツ

1 走って息が切れた。
2 今は毎週末ボーリングに行きます。
3 エアロビクスは最近非常に人気があります。
4 ジムに行って2,3時間運動します。
5 彼は毎日ジョギングをします。
6 私は空手で黒帯を持っています。
7 来週のレースには,いい調子で臨めますか？
8 彼は体育館で私の兄弟と相撲を取った。
9 水泳クラブに属しています。
10 日本でゴルフをするのは,お金がかかる。
11 剣道をするには竹刀が必要です。
12 ボクシングを見るのが好きです。
13 弓道は西洋のアーチェリーに似ています。
14 合気道は武器を使わない武道です。
15 今のところは特に好きな選手はいません。

### (2) ワン・センテンス遅れ通訳の練習

## 合気道

　私が初めて合気道に触れたのは13歳の時でした。『和の道』という名前の本を手に入れました。人が空中を飛んでいる写真を見て驚きました。そして,もっと詳しく調べてみることにしました。合気道の道場を訪ねて,入会したのです。

　合気道により私は自分を取り巻くものと,私のまわりの人々の気分を感じ取れるようになりました。この武道は私の人生となり大好きなものになったのです。将来は自分の道場を持ちたいと思っています。

## Sports 1-31

1. I lost my breath running.
2. Now I go bowling every weekend.
3. Aerobics has become very popular recently.
4. I go to the gym to work out for a few hours.
5. He goes jogging everyday.
6. I have a black belt in Karate.
7. Will you be in shape for the race next week?
8. He wrestled with my brothers in the gymnasium.
9. I belong to a swimming club.
10. It costs a lot to play golf in Japan.
11. To practice Kendo you need a bamboo sword.
12. I like watching boxing.
13. Kyudo is similar to Western archery.
14. Aikido is a martial art without weapons.
15. For the moment I don't have any favorite player.

## Aikido 1-32

My first exposure to Aikido was when I was 13. I picked up a book named "The Way of Harmony." I was fascinated by the pictures of people flying though the air. And I was inspired to take a closer look. I visited an Aikido dojo and joined them.

Aikido has made me more aware of my surroundings and the moods of people around me.

This martial art has become my life and my passion. I hope to open my dojo in the future.

## §5 ディクテーション

以下のパッセージをテキストを見ずに通して聞き，次にもう一度聞きながら下線を埋めなさい。　🅒 1-33

1  I have some happy _____. Ms. Martha Hamada is going _____. Also Martha will ____ our _____ in Tijuana, Mexico, and she will attend our monthly _____ in Mexico City. ____ _____, Martha, we hope you enjoy _____ _____.

2  There _____ today at 3 o'clock. We will _____ budget. Mr. Krueger and Ms. Beverly Kimura will be our _____. Mr. Krueger _____ _____. Ms. Kimura works at Cosmo Research. They will be talking _____ _____. The meeting will end at 5 o'clock. There will be _____ at 4:00. Both mid and _____ will attend. Thank you.

3  Ladies and gentlemen, _____ our next speaker. He _____. He is the President of BioTech industries. _____, research is _____ _____. Profits have increased _____. BioTech has become _____ _____. Let's welcome Mr. Ryu Yamakawa. He is Technology Magazine's _____.

まず全センテンスを頭ごなし翻訳またはサイトラし，要約通訳して下さい。

1. I have some happy news for all of you. Ms. Martha Hamada is going to be our new assistant sales chief. Also Martha will lead our branch office in Tijuana, Mexico, and she will attend our monthly board meetings in Mexico City. Congratulations, Martha, we hope you enjoy your new challenge.

2. There will be a budget meeting today at 3 o'clock. We will discuss next year's budget. Mr. Krueger and Ms. Beverly Kimura will be our guest speakers. Mr. Krueger is famous as an expert on finance. Ms. Kimura works at Cosmo Research. They will be talking about tax problems that affect our company. The meeting will end at 5 o'clock. There will be a 10 minute break at 4:00. Both mid and top level managers will attend. Thank you.

3. Ladies and gentlemen, it's time to introduce our next speaker. He is known to all of you. He is the President of BioTech industries. Under his leadership, research is twice as big as before. Profits have increased over 20%.
BioTech has become a world leader in the fight against children's diseases. Let's welcome Mr. Ryu Yamakawa. He is Technology Magazine's Man of the Year.

# Lesson 8

## §1 クイック・レスポンス

(1) ボキャビル

**演習方法**

日本語と英語の合成語を2秒以内で発音します。
次に日本語から英語，英語から日本語へ即時変換して下さい。

## Business & Communication 1

| | | |
|---|---|---|
| 1 | 当局 | authorities |
| 2 | 備品 | supplies |
| 3 | 改良 | improvement |
| 4 | 修復 | renovation |
| 5 | 革新 | innovation |
| 6 | 減少 | reduction |
| 7 | 景気後退 | recession |
| 8 | 豊富な | opulent |
| 9 | ぶらぶら歩き | stroll(ed) |
| 10 | 〜のまん中に | amidst |
| 11 | 壮大な | grand |
| 12 | 孤児院 | orphanage |
| 13 | 以前に | previously |
| 14 | 牧師 | pastor |
| 15 | 監禁する | imprison(ed) |
| 16 | 尋問する | interrogate(d) |
| 17 | 独房 | cell(s) |
| 18 | 墓場 | graveyard |
| 19 | 政権 | regime |
| 20 | 栄養失調の | malnourished |

(2) **数字**　英語に変換して下さい。

56万，5千，56万5千，98万，6千，98万6千，
88万2千，79万，6百，79万6百，85万，
90万1千，99万9900，99万9999，100万，
120万，199万，34万5千，134万5千6百，
120万÷5千＝24，120,000 divided by 5,000 equals 24.

## §2　リテンションとリプロダクション

(1) **リテンション練習**
数回音読して暗唱して下さい。　　　　　　　🄯 1-34

A　Things don't seem to be going well under the new management.
B　The reasons are related to resentment from the floor employees. The restructuring methods they implemented caused the people to distrust the management.
A　What could they do to improve the situation?
B　They will have to start to listen to the voices from the floor.

(2) **リプロダクション**
日本語文を読み，または聞き，即時に訳出して下さい。

A　新しい経営陣のもとで何かうまくいってないようですね。
B　フロアの従業員が恨みに思うことがあるのです。
　　会社の取ったリストラのやり方が経営陣に対しての不信を生んでしまったのです。
A　状況改善に何か出来るでしょうか？
B　フロアの人々の意見を聞くようにしなければなりませんね。

## §3 区切り聞き

**演習方法**

初回は区切り聞きでリピーティング，二回目は該当部の日本語訳を音読して下さい。三回目から自分の言葉で通訳して下さい。

# Communication 1

1-35
E. Jannetta

| | |
|---|---|
| Vienna was the meeting place. | ウィーンが集合場所でした。 |
| It seemed so casually opulent | 気張らない豊かさにあふれて |
| as people strolled in sunshine | 人々は日光をあびながら |
| amidst grand buildings | 壮大な建物の間をそぞろ歩いたり |
| or sat at street cafes | 通りのカフェに座って |
| to watch the world | 見ています |
| leisurely pass by ; it could be nothing but a contrast | 世界がゆったり移って行くのを，それはまさに対照的でした |
| to the final destination of my trip : an orphanage | 私の旅の最終目的地とはそれは孤児院で |
| in the northeast of Romania. | ルーマニアの北東部にあるのです。 |
| Yet that was not the real beginning of my journey. | でもそれは旅の本当の始まりではなかったのでした。 |
| It had started | 始まったのは |
| four years previously | それより四年前 |
| during time spent in India; | インドにいたときです |
| there I had come across writings | 書物に出会ったのです |
| by Richard Wurmbrand, | リチャード・ウルムブランドの。 |
| a Romanian pastor | 彼はルーマニア人の牧師で |
| who had been imprisoned | ずっと投獄されていたのです。 |
| for having Christian faith | キリストへの信仰を持っていた |
| in a communist country. | から共産主義の国で |

| | |
|---|---|
| He was sent | 彼は送られました |
| to the most feared prison | ルーマニアで最も恐れられていた |
| in Romania | 監獄に |
| to be interrogated and beaten. | そこで尋問され打たれました |
| His account of Romania | 彼のルーマニア記事は |
| and of these specific experiences | 具体的な経験で |
| opened up a door | ドアを開けてくれました |
| in my imagination | 想像上でですが, |
| to a world | 未知の世界に向かって扉を |
| I had little knowledge of. | 開けたのです。 |
| We crossed the border | 私たちは国境を越えて |
| into Romania. | ルーマニアに入りました |
| As we drove past the actual | かの監獄を車で通り過ぎるとき |
| prison where Wurmbrand had | 牧師が捕まっていた場所に |
| been held and saw the graveyard | 墓地がありました |
| for the former prisoners of the | 独房に収容されたかつての囚人達の |
| cells. | ために。 |
| I saw the concrete reality of | 体制の具体的事実を見ました |
| a regime which had allowed | 殆ど自由を許さなかったのです |
| little freedom to its people. | その国民に対して。 |
| Having large families was | 大家族が |
| encouraged by the government | 政府により奨励されましたが |
| but such a freedom resulted | この自由の結果 |
| in children of poor families | 貧しい家の子供達は |
| becoming malnourished. | 栄養失調になりました。 |
| Many of these children | これらの多くは |
| were given up to orphanages | 孤児院に送られました |
| since parents could not afford | 両親がどうにも |
| to keep them. | 出来なかったからです。 |

## §4　商談通訳

初回はサイトラして同時通訳の訳出パターンを検討して下さい。次に即時変換練習を行って下さい。

### 情報交換　　　　　　　　　1-36

**BP**　Now I'd like to tell you about our current situation. First let me give you some background information.

**KS**　お願いいたします。

**BP**　Our company was founded in 1929. We manufacture cameras and microscopes, and a variety of optical devices and equipment. At present we are the 6th largest producer of photographic equipment in the country, and in the near future we are planning to expand our business in the production of calculators and other business machines.

**KS**　主要工場はどこにあるのですか。

**BP**　We have factories in 3 countries. One is in Canada, one in the States, and we have another one in Mexico. We employ a total of 32,000 people.

**KS**　私の理解するところですと，サムソン・カメラさんは買収によって東アジアに事業拡張をなさる予定ですね。

**BP**　Yes, our main focus is to establish a factory in Taiwan to manufacture microscope parts.

|商談通訳|

## Exchanging information

BP＝Brian Pillman　　Samson Camera, Inc.（サムソンカメラ）
KS＝Ken Sasaki　　　Hokuto Trading Co.（北斗商事株式会社）

**BP** 現在の状況についてお話ししましょう。まず背景説明を差し上げます。

**KS** Yes, thank you.

**BP** 弊社は1929年に創立され，カメラ及び顕微鏡並びに種々の光学機器の製造に携わっております。現在は国内では第六位のカメラ・メーカーです。そして近い将来には計算機とその他のビジネス機器の製造にビジネスを拡張する予定です。

**KS** Where are your main factories?

**BP** 3か国にあります。一つがカナダ，一つがアメリカ，そしてもう一つがメキシコです。総従業員数32,000人です。

**KS** As I understand it, Samson Camera is planning to expand into East Asia through acquisition.

**BP** はい，私どもの狙いは台湾に顕微鏡の部品工場を設立することです。

## §5 速読練習

リーディング・スピードを測定して下さい。

# The Magic of Nahnningi Island (Ponape)

1-37
A. Goodman

My cottage faces East and looks directly onto the reef and the open ocean beyond. A breadfruit tree close by is home to a golden plover who is supposed to be nesting in the forests of Siberia but seems to have forgotten his family responsibilities. Has he become a beachcomber, too, I wonder? In Ponapean he is the "kulu", and what a virtuoso of a songbird he is! When he bursts into song in his old breadfruit tree by the shore, his little piccolo trills and the rich warbling melodies are the sweetest music in all Ponape.

Within sight of my cottage lies the deep pool of Kutun, the reef god. It is the deepest pool on the entire reef and is the only place on the reef's edge where the long ocean rollers subside and smooth over in deference to the god. In this strange, submarine sanctuary lives the black and yellow-banded fish, —lord of the pool.

The kulu bird is protected by a beachcomber's taboo. Just listen to him celebrating matins in the breadfruit tree! And he flies off to make a meal of those tiny darting flashes of silver down there in the shallows where a reef heron is solemnly promenading. Oh, and I almost forgot to mention the papaya, freshly picked and cut up into crescents of soft, orange flesh.

You have to be quick to spot the two crimson flashes as a pair of lorykeets fly through the palms overhead. These little parrots with purple heads, dark red bodies and a dash of green and yellow in their tail and wings, relish the fruit of the garden.

## Nocturne

Night falls swiftly on Nahnningi. We have already lost the sun and, for a brief moment, the palms are silhouetted black against the pale afterglow.

Nowhere do stars appear in such awesome numbers as in this Ponapean night sky. The largest of them are so close they mingle with the palms as if to share their reverie. Sung to rest by the music of the reef, how softly they sleep, our beachcomber and the kulu bird, and how sweetly they dream!

Eco-thinking is not an entirely new concept for Ponapeans. Like other Pacific islanders, Ponapeans are born into a totemic fellowship and live under the sign of one or other of the bird or fish species.

Have you ever experienced in the weirdest of dreams the strange sensation of feeling all your teeth loose in your mouth? Well, according to Ponapeans, that is what will happen to you if you eat dolphin meat, your teeth will drop out!

Dolphins themselves believe they are our kinsmen and treat us accordingly. You can depend on them to come to your rescue if you are attacked by a shark. For a dolphin to behave indifferently towards us would be unbrotherly of him and undolphinlike. Conversely, for humans to catch a dolphin and kill him or worse, put him in a circus and make an acrobat of him, would be callous and inhumane.

The Japanese feel instinctively at home in Ponape. They see residual signs everywhere of Japanese rule and habitation. The old-time feasts of Japanese Ponape are legendary and are still remembered by elderly people.

# Lesson 9

## §1 クイック・レスポンス

(1) ボキャビル

**演習方法**

日本語と英語の合成語を2秒以内で発音します。
次に日本語から英語，英語から日本語へ即時変換して下さい。

## Business & Communication 2

| | | |
|---|---|---|
| 1 | 収入 | revenue |
| 2 | 身の回り品 | personal effects |
| 3 | 分析 | analysis |
| 4 | 不可抗力 | force majeure |
| 5 | 職長 | foreman |
| 6 | 特許 | patent |
| 7 | 委任状 | power of attorney |
| 8 | 品質管理 | quality control |
| 9 | ユーティリティ，光熱費 | utilities |
| 10 | 下水 | sewage |
| 11 | 思いつく | conceive |
| 12 | 基金，資金 | fund |
| 13 | からなる | consist of |
| 14 | 配給する，配る | distribute |
| 15 | 一致 | unity |
| 16 | くぎる | punctuate(d) |
| 17 | ヒマワリ | sunflower |
| 18 | みがく | burnish(ed) |
| 19 | 衝突する | clash(ed) |
| 20 | まき散らす | scatter |

(2) **数字** 英語に変換して下さい。

100万, 200万, 50万, 250万, 300万, 10万,
310万, 500万, 20万, 520万, 600万, 25万,
625万, 725万, 845万, 955万, 150万, 1万

## §2 リテンションとリプロダクション

(1) **リテンション練習**
数回音読して暗唱して下さい。　　　　　　1-39

A　We are very much interested in concluding the technical assistance agreement with you.
B　Good. Then we should start to discuss the details so that our lawyer can make up a draft for both of us.
A　Fine. Our stance is that we'd like to have a short-term agreement of 2 years at first. And if the results are satisfactory, we'll extend the term for 3 more years.
B　Frankly speaking, a short-term project is not convenient for us.

(2) **リプロダクション**
英語に変換して下さい。

A　私どもは御社との技術援助契約に興味を持っております。
B　それはどうも。では細部についての協議を始めて、後に私どもの弁護士に双方の草案を作成してもらいましょう。
A　結構です。私どもとしてはまず短期の2年の契約を結びたいと存じます。そしてもし満足の行く成果があがれば3年間延長をする所存です。
B　率直に申し上げると、短期のプロジェクトは私どもにとっては都合がよくないのです。

## §3 区切り聞き

**演習方法**

初回の区切り聞きでリピーティング，二回目は該当部の日本語訳を音読し，三回目からは自分の言葉で通訳して下さい。

### Communication 2　　🄵 1-40

| | |
|---|---|
| The idea of the orphanage had been conceived of | 孤児院のアイデアは |
| three years earlier | 3年前 |
| by a Romanian pastor | ルーマニアの牧師が考えたもので |
| who had escaped from Romania | 彼はルーマニアから |
| in 1974 to return with | 1974年に逃亡し戻ったのは |
| the end of communist rule. | 共産主義支配が終わってからでした。 |
| Funded by international | 資金は国際的な |
| Christian organizations | キリスト教組織が供給し |
| it had slowly been built | ゆっくりと |
| stage by stage | 一段一段造られてゆき |
| until one year ago | 最終的に一年前 |
| the first child was admitted. | 初めての子供が入れられたのです。 |
| 　I discovered this information | この情報を発見したのは |
| on the three day trip with my | 3日間の旅行を私のチームと共に |
| team across Austria, Hungary | オーストリア，ハンガリーと |
| and Romania. | ルーマニアに行ったときです。 |
| The meeting place had been Vienna, | 集合場所はウィーンで |
| the group consisting of 22 people from 4 different countries: | グループは22人から構成され 4か国から集まっていました。 |
| Austria, Germany, | オーストリア，ドイツ， |
| the U.S.A. and Britain. | アメリカとイギリスです。 |
| We were to help | 私たちは |

| | |
|---|---|
| with the completion of the orphanage | 孤児院の完成を手伝い |
| and with distributing clothes | 衣類を配給し |
| and other help to the neighbourhood. | 付近の人々を手伝うのです。 |
| We had brought | 持って行ったのは |
| supplies of medicine, | 医療品 |
| toys and books with us. | 玩具と本です。 |
|  Three days of travelling | 3日間 |
| in three minibuses | マイクロバス3台での旅は |
| was something of a journey | ちょっとしたものでしたが |
| yet it was a good opportunity | とても良い機会でした |
| not only for team unity | チームが一つになり， |
| but also for us | 私たちは |
| to come to appreciate Romania. | ルーマニアの良さを体験しました。 |
| The journey was punctuated | 旅は |
| by fields and fields of sunflowers bringing brightness | ヒマワリ畑の明るさで強調されていました。 |
| that clashed | それは |
| with the grey concrete apartment blocks of the cities. | 町の灰色のコンクリートのアパートのブロックと衝突しているような印象を与えました。 |
| | |
| A contrast too was the beauty | もう一つのコントラストは |
| of Transylvania with its green | トランシルバニアの美しさで |
| hills and scatterings of | 緑の丘があり |
| delicate flowers | 優美な花もそこここに見え |
| that added their own freshness. | 新鮮さを増していました。 |
| There was a sense | 感覚は |
| of being transported back in time to see horses and carts | 時間が昔に戻ったようでした 馬や荷車が |
| as the main form of transport. | 交通の主要な手段でした。 |

## §4　商談通訳

英文を頭ごなし翻訳（またはサイトラ）して自分なりの同時通訳の訳出パターンを検討して下さい。次に即時変換練習を行って下さい。

### 質問　1-41

S　御社の配達とサポートのシステムについて少しうかがいたいのですが。

C　Of course, please feel free to ask any questions.

S　お話によると50以上の倉庫を中央アメリカにお持ちだそうですね。商品の在庫は通常はどのくらいなのですか。

C　Over 50,000 crates.

S　私どもが必要としているサプライヤーは即納入出来、特に品不足の時にも、そう出来る業者です。

C　I can assure you that we supply regular customers as a matter of priority.

S　商品は全倉庫に均等配分されているのですか。

C　No, each country has different requirements therefore the type and quality of merchandise we stock depends on the market demands of each individual area.

S　なるほど。最後の質問です。アフター・サービスにはどの様な重点を置かれておられますか。

商談通訳

# Questions

C　Mr. Casas　　　　Latin American Warehouse
S　Ms. Shiratori　　Nippon Wholesaler's Organization

S　Can I ask you some questions about your delivery and support systems?

C　どうぞ，何でもきいて下さい。

S　You said you have over 50 warehouses throughout Central America. Could you give me an idea of how much merchandise you usually have in stock?

C　50,000 クレート以上です。

S　We need a supplier who can deliver on short notice and especially during times when there is a shortage.

C　それは大丈夫だと断言いたします。お得意様を最優先に置かせて頂いております。

S　Is all the merchandise distributed evenly in each of the warehouses?

C　いいえ。それぞれの国での必要条件が違いますので商品のタイプや質は各地域の市場の需要に従ってストックしております。

S　I see. One final question: what emphasis do you place on follow-up services?

## §5 ディクテーション

以下のパッセージをテキストを見ずに通して聞き，次にもう一度聞きながら下線部を埋めなさい。

(1) **Sumo**  ◎1-42

Another famous Japanese sport is sumo. Sumo is _____ and it _____. It is also perhaps _____ fat.
Sumo wrestlers are _____.

 To _____ a man must stand at least 5 feet 6 inches tall and _____. Those are the _____.

 Most sumo wrestlers are six feet tall or taller and _____ _____.

 They wear only a loincloth _____. The ring is _____ _____ and _____.

 The _____ is to throw, _____ _____, or cause some part of his body _____ of his feet to _____ of the ring.

 During the _____ just before _____, the wrestlers throw _____. Salt in Japan _____ and it is _____ sacred.

 _____ each year for wrestlers from various _____ teams.

要約して下さい。

(1) **Sumo**

Another famous Japanese sport is sumo. Sumo is Japan's national sport and it can be called a type of wrestling. It is also perhaps the only sport in the world in which the paticipants deliberately eat to get fat.
Sumo wrestlers are not classed according to weight.

To qualify as a sumo wrestler a man must stand at least 5 feet 6 inches tall and weigh at least 165 pounds. Those are the minimum requirements.
Most sumo wrestlers are six feet tall or taller and weigh somewhere between 250 and 350 pounds.

They wear only a loincloth in the ring. The ring is 15 feet in diameter and outlined by a thick straw rope.

The object of the sport is to throw, push the opponent out of the ring, or cause some part of his body other than the soles of his feet to touch the earthen floor of the ring.

During the warming up exercises just before a match, the wrestlers throw a handful of salt into the ring. Salt in Japan stands for purity and it is considered sacred.

Six tournaments are held each year for wrestlers from various stables forming east and west teams.

# Lesson 10

## §1 クイック・レスポンス

(1) ボキャビル

**演習方法**

日本語と英語の合成語を2秒以内で発音します。
次に日本語から英語，英語から日本語へ即時変換して下さい。

## Business & Communication 3

| | | |
|---|---|---|
| 1 | 経営陣 | management |
| 2 | 売掛金 | account receivable |
| 3 | 頭金 | down payment |
| 4 | 忠誠 | loyalty |
| 5 | パンフレット | brochure |
| 6 | 共同組合 | cooperative |
| 7 | 定期購読者 | subscriber |
| 8 | 提案制 | suggestion system |
| 9 | 機会均等 | equal opportunity |
| 10 | 見積もり額 | quotations |
| 11 | 譲歩する | concede |
| 12 | の点から | in terms of |
| 13 | 組合 | union |
| 14 | 経費 | expenses |
| 15 | 倒産する | go bankrupt |
| 16 | 障壁 | barrier |
| 17 | 悩ませる | perturb |
| 18 | 表情に表して | demonstrative |
| 19 | 信じられない | incredible |
| 20 | 超越する | transcend |

(2) **数字** 英語に変換して下さい。

200万，50万，250万，300万，15万，315万，
500万，150万，19万，900万，1,000万，2000万

## §2 リテンションとリプロダクション

(1) **リテンション練習**
数回音読して暗唱して下さい。　　　　　　　1-43

A　Your quotations are too high for us. I'm afraid we'll start looking somewhere else. Isn't there any possibility for you to concede in terms of prices and payment conditions?
B　We're ready to listen to you. Please tell us the prices and terms you want.
A　OK. Our position is that we want at least a 35% discount and 2 payments a year, in June and in December.
B　I see. It's a tough question. I think we have to discuss it on our side. Could we take a 15 minute break?

(2) **リプロダクション**
日本語文を読み，または聞き，即時に訳出して下さい。

A　御社の見積もりは高過ぎます。これでは他をあたらなければなりません。価格と支払い条件の点で譲歩の余地はないのでしょうか？
B　お話を伺う用意はあります。御社が希望される価格と条件をお聞かせ下さい。
A　そうですね。私どもとしては少なくとも35％の割引と支払いは年2回，6月と12月が希望です。
B　なるほど。難しい問題ですね。当方は協議しなければなりません。15分休憩したいと思います。

## §3 区切り聞き

**演習方法**

初回の区切り聞きでリピーティング，二回目は該当部の日本語訳を音読，三回目からはリテンションをしながら自分の言葉で通訳します。

## Communication 3  1-44

| | |
|---|---|
| As we drove into the small village where the orphanage was many of the people we passed by smiled and waved. | 小さい村に車で行くと そこに孤児院があったので 大勢の人達は 私たちが通りかかると ほほ笑んで手を振ってくれました。 |
| The children too were very welcoming when we finally arrived at our destination. | 子供たちも大歓迎してくれました やっと目的地に着いたときに。 |
| Although they had only been in the orphanage for a few months, the children had already become so used to teams like ours coming from other European countries, Japan and the U.S.A. that they were natural cases for internationalization. | 彼等は入りました 孤児院に2，3か月前に ですが，子供たちはもう 慣れていました 私たちのようなチームが 他のヨーロッパの国々や 日本やアメリカから来るのに それで自然に 国際的になっていたのです。 |
| They were so accepting of people who could not speak Romanian but who could smile, hug, play games and sing songs that language became no barrier. | 人々を簡単に受け入れ ルーマニア語を話せなくても ほお笑むことができ，抱き締め， ゲームをし，歌を歌い 言語は障壁にはなりませんでした。 |
| The children seemed so unperturbed by my English replies | 子供達も全然悩むことなく 私が英語で答えても |

| | |
|---|---|
| to their steady flow of Romanian. | 彼等のルーマニア語は止まりません |
| It was just enough to communicate | 意思伝達は充分でした |
| in the language of friendship. | 友情の言語が使われましたから。 |
| This was true also | 同じことが |
| for the Romanian kitchen staff | ルーマニア人の台所のスタッフ |
| of the orphanage | にも言えました |
| who spoke little English. | 彼等のほとんどは英語が出来ず |
| They showed kindness in their | やさしさで |
| care of us and in their demonstrative greetings. | 私たちの世話をしてくれ表情に表して挨拶してくれました。 |
| Among my team members | 私のチームのメンバーに |
| there was one lady from Germany who could speak neither Romanian nor English but the heart she had for the children and for those in the neighbourhood spoke more than words ever could ; in her real ability to develop friendships with the Romanian people was an incredible example of concern and love being communicated. | ドイツ人の女性がいましたルーマニア語も英語も話せませんでした。でも心は子供たちや近所の人達に言葉以上に通じたのです彼女のやりかたで友情をルーマニアの人達と築きました驚くような良い例です気遣いと愛が伝わるということの。 |
| Another kind of language : | もう一つの言語 |
| probably the best form of communication that can transcend culture, tradition, | それは多分一番良い形のコミュニケーションでそれは文化, 伝統, |
| words and experience. | 言葉と経験を超越出来るのです。 |

## §4　商談通訳

英文を頭ごなし翻訳（またはサイトラ）して自分なりの同時通訳の訳出パターンを検討して下さい。次に即時変換練習を行って下さい。

### 値引き交渉　1　　　🔘1-45

**HH**　過去二年間取引をさせて頂き，私は固定客ですね。そこでうかがいたいのですが御社の価格の見直しを考えていただけるでしょうか。

**MS**　I'll tell you what. We'd be able to offer you a much greater discount if you ordered 200 lots a month.

**HH**　正直申しまして，現時点ではキャパシティーも，そのように多大な買入れを保証する能力もありません。一か月に150ロットを注文する用意はございますが。

**MS**　Well unfortunately I'm afraid we are unable to offer any more than the regular 20% discount for purchases below 200 lots per month.

**HH**　20％の割引でしたらどこの卸売業者からでも取引関係を建てずに受けることが出来ます。ご存じのように，もう一店舗東京に開店する計画が進行中なのです。
その後でなら御社のルビーに対しての注文を保証出来ます。但し，勿論，それにはより大きい割引がいただけることが条件です。

**MS**　In that case, I'd propose guaranteed orders of rubies worth 30 million yen over a year. Could you manage that?

商談通訳

# Bargaining 1

MS ＝Mick Singh, Wholesaler in Jewelry（宝石御売業者）
HH ＝Hiroko Hasei, Retailer（小売業者）

**HH** We have been doing business for 2 years and I am a regular, I'd like to know if you would consider readjusting your prices.

**MS** さてと，より大きい割引をご提供出来るのは月に200ロットの注文をいただける場合です。

**HH** To be honest, at present we do not have the capacity or the capability to guarantee such a substantial purchase. We'd be prepared to increase our order to 150 lots per month.

**MS** 残念ですが，月に200ロット以下の注文には通常の20％以上はご提供出来かねるのです。

**HH** We can get 20% discount from any wholesaler even without the establishment of a business relationship. As you know, plans are currently underway to open another store in Tokyo. We would then be able to guarantee more purchase orders on rubies from you; on the condition, of course, that you offer us a larger discount.

**MS** その場合でしたら，私の提案は年額3,000万円以上にルビーの注文を保証して頂くことです。それでいかがでしょう。

## §5 音読またはサイトラ練習

# IRAN
**C. Dashtestani**

For many people the country of Iran calls forth an image of Ayatollah Khomeini, a war with Iraq and Muslim women clad in a dark tent-like covering. Many people recall the oil-flowing days of the last Shah of Iran. Mohammed Reza Pahlavi. For some people Iran will always be the Persia of the ancient cities of Isfahan and Persepolis, the poets Ferdowsi and Khayyam, hand-woven carpets and an ancient tradition of overwhelming hospitality.

I am one of the fortunate people who have more than one nationality. It is from the perspective of my Iranian nationality that I shall be talking a little about a country I love. We owned a property on the Caspian coast where the summer weather was very similar to that of Tokyo. If anything, it was even more humid than Tokyo. The early mornings always seemed a little more comfortable as we sat in the newly watered garden eating our breakfast.

Food plays an important part in the daily life of an Iranian. It is said that to share food with a guest is a gift from God. There is never a formal table setting as the household rarely knows how many people will be eating. I do not recall ever sitting down to a meal without at least two or more guests. Even the poorest family will offer food and one had to be very careful not to offend by refusing, to eat enough to praise the expertise of the cook yet leave enough for the family.

Our main home was in Tehran, capital of Iran. Here everything was more modern according to western standards. Instead of the traditional 'korsi' which is exactly like the Japanese 'kotatsu' we had central oil heating. Many of the modern homes now have western style toilets as well as the traditional Iranian toilet which is exactly like a traditional Japanese toilet except for two things. Instead of paper, Iranians use either a jug of water, or a type of water hose and, the toilet must never face the same direction as Mecca which is the religious centre for all Muslims.

The walls of Iranian homes tend to be very thick, the rooms large and the floors made of marble. The floors are covered with carpets that have sometimes taken years to weave. Although the homes are generally furnished with western style furniture, Iranians often sit cross-legged on the floor and whenever there are extra guests, a thick tablecloth is spread over a carpet and the food laid out somewhat like a picnic. Although these carpets have been made by hand, they are really tough.

A good carpet was always brushed clear of dust in one direction never vacuum cleaned. As in Japan, people are expected to take off their shoes before entering a house.

The climate in Tehran is very different from the climate in the Caspian area. Summers in Tehran are extremely hot, dry and dusty. For me, winter was my favourite season in Tehran. The skies would be the clearest, brightest blue, the flat rooftops of the houses and the dusty streets would be deep in snow.

A few years ago, we had a particularly heavy fall of snow in Kanagawa and I was so happy because it reminded me of those times in Tehran.

# Lesson 11

## §1 クイック・レスポンス

(1) ボキャビル

**演習方法**

本章から"negotiate―交渉する"の順番でも練習して下さい。

英語と日本語の合成語を2秒以内で発音します。

次に日本語から英語，英語から日本語へ即時変換して下さい。

## Business & Sports Communication 1

| | | |
|---|---|---|
| 1 | negotiate | 交渉する |
| 2 | provided | 但し，という条件で |
| 3 | make payments | 支払う |
| 4 | go along with | うまくやる |
| 5 | summarize | 要約する |
| 6 | Board | 重役会 |
| 7 | commencing | 始まる |
| 8 | transaction | 取引 |
| 9 | contract | 契約 |
| 10 | complaint | 苦情 |
| 11 | pitch | 投球 |
| 12 | physical | 身体の |
| 13 | gyration | 回転 |
| 14 | on the sidelines | 傍観するだけで |
| 15 | jargon | 専門語 |
| 16 | tag | タッチアウトすること（野球） |
| 17 | non-verbal | 言葉にならない |
| 18 | scratch(es) | 引っかく |
| 19 | predetermine | 先決する |
| 20 | bunt(s) | バント |

(2) **数字**　英語に変換して下さい。

55万，100万，250万，550万，1000万，2000万，
2500万，4,000万，4,400万，450万，4,450万，1億
700万，7億，7000万，70万，7000，7億700万

## §2　リテンションとリプロダクション

(1) **リテンション練習**
数回音読して暗唱して下さい。　　　　　　　　　🄯2-1

A  As soon as we start to install the machines, we'll let you know that you can send over a technical advisor.
B  I would say it's better that we decide now as to the time. It takes a bit of time to select a person. And we have to provide the person with language training.
A  I see. Then how about in mid-May.
B  That seems fine with us, too. We can start to have the new manual translated by then.

(2) **リプロダクション**
日本語文を読み，または聞き，即時に訳出して下さい。

A  機械を据つけ始めたらすぐ，お知らせします。そして技術顧問をお送り頂きます。
B  むしろ今その時期を決定したほうがよいでしょう。人材を選出するのに時間が少々かかります。そして，その者に語学トレーニングを受けさせなければなりません。
A  なるほど，では，五月中旬ではいかがでしょう。
B  結構です。それまでには新しいマニュアルの翻訳を始められます。

## §3 区切り聞き

### 演習方法

初回の区切り聞きでリピーティング，二回目は該当部の日本語訳を音読して下さい。三回目から自分の言葉で通訳して下さい。

## Sports Communication 1

2-2
S. Heverly

| | |
|---|---|
| Have you ever watched | 見たことがありますか。 |
| a sports event | スポーツ・イベントで |
| and seen people making | 人々が |
| all kinds of physical gyrations | 色々な動きをするのを |
| on the sidelines, | 試合に出場していないのに。 |
| or listened to a coach or athlete | コーチや選手が話すのを聞いて |
| speaking and felt they're speaking a foreign language? | 彼等が話しているのは外国語だと感じたことはありますか。 |
| It's all something called | それがいわゆる |
| sports communication. | スポーツ・コミュニケーションです。 |
| Each sport has its own jargon | 全てのスポーツには専門語があります。 |
| that basically can be understood | それは基本的には |
| only by those that are involved | それらに何らかの関係がある人々 |
| in the sport in some way. | のみの間でわかるというものです。 |
| For example, | 例えば |
| if you heard a baseball player talking about | もし野球の選手が |
| how he should have "slid home", | 『ホームに滑り込むべきだった』と言った時は， |
| it meant he should have tried | それは |
| to score a run by sliding | 滑り込んで |
| under the catcher's tag | キャッチャーのタッチをくぐり |

at home plate.　　　　　　　　ホーム・プレートに戻りスコアを稼
　　　　　　　　　　　　　　　ぐことを意味します。

　Lets begin with the easiest,　まず，初めに一番やさしい
physical communication.　　　体を使ったコミュニケーションを見
　　　　　　　　　　　　　　　ましょう。

　Well, one of the most often　さて，
seen　　　　　　　　　　　　　一番良く見かける
forms of nonverbal communi-　言葉以外のコミュニケーション
cation is in the sport of baseball.　は野球にあります。
When a player is batting　　　バッターは
he looks at the third basecoach　三塁のコーチを見て
to get a nonverbal signal　　　無言のシグナルを受けます
of what the manager has　　　監督が彼にして貰いたいことを
communicated
he wants the batter to do.　　これで伝えるのです。
The third base coach goes　　三塁のコーチは
through a set of signals　　　サインの一連を
that sometimes looks as if　　あたかも
he must have ants crawling　　アリが
all over his body inside his　　ユニフォームの中にはいずっている
uniform.　　　　　　　　　　　ようにしてみせます。

He touches his shoulder,　　　肩にさわり，
taps his leg,　　　　　　　　　脚を叩き
shakes one or both arms,　　片手や両手を振り
does just about everything　　色々なことを
in the third base coaching box.　三塁のコーチの席で行います。
The batter watches this scene　バッターはこのシーンを見て
and must pick-up
a predetermined sign　　　　　あらかじめ，決めてあったサインを理
to decide what to do.　　　　　解して行動します。

## §4　商談通訳

　英文を頭ごなし翻訳，又はサイトラして自分なりの同時通訳の訳出パターンを検討して下さい。次にメモを取りながら日英両語のウィスパリング通訳の演習をして下さい。

### 値引き交渉　2　　🎧 2-3

**HH**　もし割引を30％にしていただけたらルビーを2,500万円買えると思います。

**MS**　I think we'd have to negotiate further, provided you make your payments in Japanese yen.

**HH**　それでよろしいでしょう。もう一度合意事項を概括してみます。
　　　御社の割引は30％となります，時期は来春，つまり4月に。

**MS**　Exactly.

**HH**　そして，私どもとしてはパーツを150ロットとルビーを2,500万円年間で購入する。支払いは日本円で行う。

**MS**　That's correct.

**HH**　サファイアに対しては価格の点が未決です。何らかの動きが取れるのは，重役会で御社の提案を協議してからです。

**MS**　Fine.

**HH**　次回はサファイアの件と来年向けの新しいデザインの協議をいたしましょう。全てをカバーしましたっけ？

**MS**　Yes, that seems to be all. One more thing I'd appreciate it very much if you could bring the new catalogues for the winter collections.

**HH**　OKです。そういたします。

商談通訳

# Bargaining 2

MS ＝Mick Singh, Wholesaler（卸し売り業者）
HH ＝Hiroko Hasei, Retailer（小売業者）

HH　If you increased the discount to 30%, we'd buy rubies worth 25 million yen.
MS　私どももほり下げた交渉をしなければなりませんね。もっとも御社が日本円で支払って下さればという条件ですが。

HH　I think we could go along with that. So let me summarize our agreement. You will give us a 30% discount commencing next spring that is April.
MS　その通りです。
HH　And from our side, we agree to buy 150 lots of parts and rubies worth 25 million yen a year. With payments made in Japanese yen.
MS　そうです。
HH　As for sapphires, the question of pricing remains to be decided. We will be ready to work something out after I discuss your proposal with our Board.
MS　結構です。

HH　So next time we'll discuss the sapphire issue as well as the new designs for the next year. Have I covered everything?
MS　はい，それで全部です。それから，出来ましたら，冬期コレクションのカタログをお持ちいただければ大変有難いのですが。

HH　OK. I'll do that.

§5 速読またはサイトラ練習

## The Pulse of the Mothership

N. Walker

Let me begin by sharing a memory with you. A memory that has become ethereal and dreamlike over the passage of time and yet it relates only back to last summer.

I was watching the finale of a world music event which was being staged at the Confucian Temple in Ochanomizu. The Ainu folkies had played their set as had the Tokyo new-agers and so had the headliners; the Ugandan Percussion combo. Finally all the musicians joined together on the stage for the customary final jam. The mood was joyful yet serene. Suddenly a young boy aged about five jumped away from his mother's hold and danced deliriously and ecstatically on the main stage, wonderfully free from the self-consciousness of adulthood. Actually I wanted to join him but visions of me being let away to a psychiatric ward made me think twice. It did however force me to consider the awesome power of music as both a mood altering medium and as a means of inter-cultural communication which has an emotional range second to none.

Generally speaking, music knows no cultural or geopolitical borders. Why is this? To my regret I have never formally studied music. So my conclusions are unscientific to say the least. All of us seem to be led by some primeval code, to beauty, sonic or visual. Some anthropologists maintain that human beings used percussion to communicate non-verbally before the development of speech. Many others maintain that the mother's heartbeat in the womb accounts for many a teenager's passion for the reassuring rhythmic patterns of pop music. Many theorists place importance on the ancestral memories of the sound based rituals of prehistory. The answers to this question are so byzantine in their complexity, involving as they do sound waves, psychology, anthropology, history and many other disciplines that even a half-adequate answer could not find space here.

Perhaps it is dangerous to analyze too closely such an exquisite art form for fear of losing its essence. When a journalist asked Louis Armstrong what jazz was his oft-quoted reply was, "If you have to ask, you'll never know". The sentiment of that answer expresses my feelings about looking for quantitative answers about music generally.

Let us then marvel at the facts rather than question. Music can ; communicate : love, affection, awe, anger, pain, regret, wistfulness, joy and almost every other emotion we can feel. Music can perforate thick walls of cultural and national chauvinism more effectively than diplomacy ever could. We use music, individually and collectively to assuage unhappiness and grief, to enhance celebration, to give life to social events.

What I do know is that on that hot summer's day I felt joyfully happy and liberated from all the pressures of being a 20th century urban worker-ant. And I felt a warm skinship with every other fragile human being in my field of vision. Nobody denies the power of music but it is nice to be reminded of it in a world that is often brutal and dispiriting. For all our selfish and destructive stupidity the human race has created a spirit out of sound waves that is indestructible.

# Lesson 12

## §1 クイック・レスポンス

(1) ボキャビル

**演習方法**

英語と日本語の合成語を2秒以内で発音します。
次に日本語から英語，英語から日本語へ即時に変換して下さい。

## Business & Sports Communication 2

| | | |
|---|---|---|
| 1 | bond | 債券 |
| 2 | securities | 証券 |
| 3 | warrant | 保証 |
| 4 | CPA | 公認会計士 |
| 5 | CEO | 最高経営責任者 |
| 6 | subsidiary | 子会社 |
| 7 | stock | 株，在庫 |
| 8 | share | 株 |
| 9 | shareholder | 株主 |
| 10 | general assembly | 総会 |
| 11 | crouch | 身をかがめる |
| 12 | chatter | おしゃべり |
| 13 | inspiring | 鼓舞する |
| 14 | confidence | 確信 |
| 15 | apologize | 謝る |
| 16 | swing | 振る |
| 17 | rally | 急上昇 |
| 18 | submit | 提出する |
| 19 | court | 裁判所 |
| 20 | up and coming | 有望な |

(2) **数字**　英語に変換して下さい。

5000万，5500万，4000万，4700万，6000万，8900万，
1億，3億，5億，10億，15億，6億，4000万，400万，
1億3000万，1億3000万，3億5000万，3億5000万，
200万，1万，15万，4000万，14億，60億，65億10万

## §2　リテンションとリプロダクション

(1) **リテンション練習**
数回音読して暗唱して下さい。　　　　　　　　　　🄯2-5

A　We found your model is superior to others in terms of maneuverability and adaptability. But after running it in our tests, we're concerned with the durability.
B　With proper maintenance, that shouldn't be any problem.
A　Also, it's been pointed out by our engineers that we do not need other functions besides cutting. If you can take extra accessories off, there should be a large difference in price.

(2) **リプロダクション練習**
日本語文を読み，または聞き，即時に訳出して下さい。

A　御社のモデルは他社のものより優秀で，操作性と適応性が優れています。しかしテストしてみると耐久性について懸念があります。
B　適切な保守点検があればその心配はないでしょう。
A　また，エンジニアから指摘があったのですが，当社では裁断以外，他の機能が必要がないのです。もし，余分な付属品を外していただけたら価格の点で大きな違いがでるはずです。

## §3　区切り聞き

**演習方法**

初回は区切り聞きでリピーティング，二回目は該当部の日本語訳を音読して下さい。三回目から自分の言葉で通訳して下さい。

## Sports Communication 2　　2-6

| | |
|---|---|
| One of the most up and coming popular sports in the world is basketball. | 一番有望で 世界で人気があるスポーツは バスケットボールです。 |
| 　Basketball has produced such colorful terms as: fast break, man-to-man, hang-time, slam dunk. | バスケットボールが産出したのは 多彩な用語で ファスト・ブレーク，マンツーマン，ハング・タイム，スラム・ダンクなどがあります。 |
| A lot of nonverbal actions have come from basketball. The sport action called the "high-5" started back in the 70's. | 言葉のないアクションの多くは バスケットボールから来ています。 スポーツ・アクションの ハイ・ファイブは 70年代に始まりました。 |
| 　The latest "hip" thing to do in basketball is the "chest slam", where 2 burly chested individuals congratulate each other by jumping up chest-to-chest. | 最新流行のものは バスケットボールでは チェスト・スラムでこれは 二人の胸のたくましい人物が 互いに祝うのに 胸と胸をあわせて飛び上がることです。 |
| 　Another sport which is extremely popular in the United States, is football, American style. In this case the ultimate score | もう一つのスポーツは 非常に人気があります。 アメリカにおいて，それは アメリカン・フットボールです。 この場合究極のスコアは |

| | |
|---|---|
| in football is a "touchdown", | フットボールではタッチダウンです。 |
| when you run or catch the ball | つまり選手は走るかボールをキャッ |
| in the "end-zone". | チします，エンドゾーンにおいて。 |
| They try to outdo each other | 互いにしのぎ合い |
| in celebrating their touchdowns | タッチダウンを祝います |
| by doing all kinds of | あらゆる |
| "touchdown" dances, | タッチダウン・ダンス， |
| flips, slides, and moonwalks. | フリップ，スライドやムーンウォーク |
|    In football | をします。フットボールでは |
| there is a lot of intimidation. | 威嚇も沢山あります |
| Much of it is verbal, | 多くは言葉によるもので |
| with yells like | 怒鳴りによる |
| "I'm gonna rip off your head!" | 『頭をもぎ取ってやるぞ。』などがそ |
| | うです。 |
|    These three sports | これらの3スポーツは |
| are the three most famous | もっとも有名な |
| team sports in America. | チームスポーツです。アメリカでは。 |
|    In individual sports | 個人スポーツ， |
| like tennis and golf | 例えばテニス，ゴルフでも |
| there is also | |
| a jargon of communication. | 専門用語があります。 |
| It's hard to find | 難しいです |
| a more fitting word | よりピッタリした語を見つけるのは |
| for a bad shot | バッドショットやスコアにたいして， |
| or score than, BOGEY! | ボギーという語のほかは。 |
| Next time you watch a sport, | 次にスポーツを観戦するときは |
| I hope you can yell things like, | 次のように叫んで下さい。 |
| "Hip, hip, hurrah!" | ヒップ，ヒップ，フレー！ |

## §4　ウィスパリング商談通訳

### (1)　ウィスパリング通訳

パッセージをサイトラして同時通訳の訳出パターンを検討して下さい。次に即時変換練習を行って下さい。

プレゼンテーションの最後　　　🄫2-7

Presenter ;
At this stage I'd like to summarize the main points.
Japanese products sold world-wide have earned a reputation for outstanding performance and quality.
This is due to an effective distribution system and high standards of quality. According to the latest survey, consumer preference for our products in the Middle Eastern countries has been higher than ever. As a result, we have decided to export more products.
In the end, this is the blueprint of our new advertising campaign. For TV commercials and magazines, we are going to feature a cute comic character.
As you can see, thorough research has been done.
We are confident that some of our new products will do very well in those markets.
Thank you for your attention, if you have any questions, please feel free.

Questioner :　Could you show us a breakdown of your advertising budget?
Presenter :　At present, I don't have the figures with me, but I can get them to you by the end of the week.
Questioner :　Could you give us more information about your export strategy?

(2) **ワン・センテンス遅れ通訳**
　　日英ウィスパリング通訳がスムーズにできるようになったら
　　ワン・センテンス遅れ訳に挑戦して下さい。

## The final part of a presentation

Presenter ;
　この段階において主要ポイントをまとめてみたいと思います。
　日本製品は世界中で売られており優れた性能と品質で定評を得ております。
その理由は効果的な流通システムと高い品質基準です。
最新の調査によると，当社製品への顧客好感度は中東諸国において益々かつてないほど高くなっています。

その結果，私どもが決定したのはより多くの製品を輸出することです。
最後にこれが当社の新広告キャンペーンの青写真です。

テレビ，コマーシャルと雑誌については，かわいいコミック・キャラクターを起用します。
　ご覧のように，綿密なリサーチがなされております。
私達は自信を持って，新製品の幾つかが中東市場でよい成績を収めるということが出来ます。
　ご静聴ありがとうございました。何かご質問がありましたらどうぞ御遠慮なくどうぞ。
Questioner :　　広告費の内訳を見せていただけますか？

Presenter :　　今，数字を手元に持ち合わせておりませんが，週の終わりまでには差し上げることが出来ます。
Questioner :　　輸出戦略についての情報をもっといただけますか？

## §5 メモ化リプロダクション

メモ化して下さい。メモをもとに聴衆に語りかけるように英語で発表して下さい。

## Religions　　　🄯2-8

　There are three main religions in Japan ― Shintoism, Buddhism and Christianity. Buddhism came to Japan in the 6th century after having spread from India through China. Christianity arrived in Japan in the 16th century.

　Shintoism is our native religion. It's a combination of nature worship and ancestor worship. It has no known founder, no fixed doctrine and nothing like a Bible.
It is a polytheistic religion developed from the primitive religions of Japan and its gods and goddess are called Kami.
Kami vary in nature from personified natural phenomena to deified people.

　As a matter of fact, most Japanese are both Buddhists and Shintoists. They get married in a Shinto ceremony but are usually buried with buddhist rituals. This duality of religious belief is quite harmonious and works out rather well.
Shintoism places emphasis on enjoying the natural life, here and now, while Buddhism stresses the life after death and the necessity of working toward a place in heaven.

## §6　要約通訳

メモを取りながら聞き，そのメモをもとに要約通訳して下さい。

### モラ氏歓送会　　　2-9

　Ben Mora has worked with us for 35 years
and we honor him today.
　When he graduated from
the University of La Paz,
Ben joined us
when we were a small company.
Universal Engineering
had a lot of competition.

　Ben's first patent
helped our finances a lot.
And our reputation grew with our size.
　Ben has always been
a great example of hard work, creativity
and thinking of others at the company first.
　His many inventions
have made him a leader,
and his fantastic attitude
and bright smile are unforgettable.

　We hope that in leaving our company
he will be starting a new life
with more freedom to do what he wants.
　Ben, you keep in touch.
　Good luck and God bless, Ben.
　Here's a toast to your health
and happiness, Ben.

# Lesson 13

## §1　クイック・レスポンス

(1) 　ボキャビル

**演習方法**

英語と日本語の合成語を2秒以内で発音します。
次に日本語から英語，英語から日本語へ即時に変換して下さい。

## "Business" & In Search of Adventure 1

| | | |
|---|---|---|
| 1 | Purchasing department | 購買部 |
| 2 | retirement | 引退 |
| 3 | pension | 年金 |
| 4 | capital | 資本 |
| 5 | entrepreneur | 企業家 |
| 6 | industrialist | 工場経営者 |
| 7 | headquarters | 本社 |
| 8 | colleague | 同僚 |
| 9 | compensation | 補償 |
| 10 | resignation | 辞職 |
| 11 | raise | 昇給 |
| 12 | promotion | 昇進 |
| 13 | luncheon | 昼食会 |
| 14 | premium | 保険料 |
| 15 | insurance policy | 保険証書 |
| 16 | atheist | 無神論者 |
| 17 | spell | 一続きの時間 |
| 18 | grim | 冷酷な |
| 19 | rage | 猛威をふるう |
| 20 | furnishing | 家具 |

(2) **数字**　英語に変換して下さい。

2億，　4億，　15億，　110億，　215億，　20億，
9億，　1000万，　9億1000万，　6億，　6000万，
2500万，　10万，　105万，　400万，　200億，　160億，
12億，　24億，　115億，　100億，　205億，　21億

## §2　リテンションとリプロダクション

### (1)　リテンション練習
　　数回音読して暗唱して下さい。　　　　　　　　　♪2-10

A　This is the luxurious type of the contemporary model.
B　To be honest with you, what I have in mind doesn't need to be this good.
A　Then, why don't you try an economical type. This is a bit smaller and comes in 4 colors.
B　I see. Could I try this?
A　Of course, please go ahead.

### (2)　リプロダクション
　　日本語文を読み，または聞き，即時に訳出してください。

A　これが現行モデルのデラックス・タイプです。
B　正直いって，私の案では，これほどよい必要はないのです。
A　では，エコノミー・タイプをご覧下さい。これは少し小さく，色が四色あります。
B　なるほど，試していいですか。
A　もちろん，どうぞ。

## §3　区切り聞き

**演習方法**

初回の区切り聞きでリピーティング，二回目は該当部の日本語訳を音読します。三回目から自分の言葉で通訳して下さい。

### In Search of Adventure 1

2-11
I. Wyness

| | |
|---|---|
| England was blanketed in snow the day a wide-eyed student left Heathrow Airport in London in search of adventure to a biblical land | イギリスは雪に覆われていました。その日，目を見張った学生はロンドンのヒースロー空港を発ち冒険を求めて聖書の国に向かいました |
| which held a curiosity for him, despite his being an atheist. | そこは彼の好奇心の的でした 彼は無神論者なのに。 |
| I was 22 years old | 私は22歳でした |
| when I decided to leave | 絶対に |
| the comfort of my family home | 家族の安楽を離れ |
| for a spell on an Israeli kibbutz (farm commune). | 一時期イスラエルにキブツ農場コミューンに行くのでした。 |
| I read about the Israeli kibbutz system as a schoolboy and wondered | キブツについて読んだのは学生の時で不思議だと思いました |
| what a classless moneyless society would be like. | 階層やお金の無い社会とはどの様なものなのかと。 |
| When I arrived | 到着したのは |
| at kibbutz Yad Mordechai, | キブツ・ヤド・モルデカイで |
| 66 kilometers south of Tel Aviv, | テル・アビブから66キロ南です |
| I was reminded | 思い出したのは |
| of the dangerous nature | 危険性です |
| of this area near the Gaza Strip | この地方はガザ地方に近く |
| as I saw numerous kibbutzniks | 大勢のキブツニク |

| | |
|---|---|
| (Israelis who live on a kibbutz) picking fruit while wearing army fatigues with automatic rifles slung over their shoulders, grim reminders of the Six Day War, dotted the landscape in the form of steel replicas of the kibbutzniks who fell during the battle that raged between Israel and Egypt, on the very spot where I stood. | つまりキブツのメンバーが果物を摘んでいるのを見たところ軍隊の作業着を着て自動小銃を肩から掛けていました，それは6日間戦争の不気味な記念品です風景に点在している鋼鉄製のレプリカでしたキブツニクで戦闘中に亡くなった人達でした。イスラエルとエジプトとの間で猛威をふるった戦闘の地に私はいたのです。 |
|    My home for the next 12 months was a group of huts surrounded by trees which gave the appearance of a German POW camp. I shared a cold, Spartan hut with 2 other volunteers. It had a stone floor with only a camp-bed and table for furnishings. | この先12か月私が住む家は小屋の一群が木に囲まれたもので外見はドイツの戦争捕虜収容所でした。冷たい，スパルタ式の小屋に他のボランティア2人と住みました。石の床とキャンプベッドとテーブルがありました。家具としてです。 |
|    It wasn't long before I was put to work in the fields picking oranges and grapefruits with a cocktail of nationalities. My team of 4 consisted of an Australian, a Swede and an Austrian. | すぐに農場で働かされオレンジやグレープフルーツを様々な国の人達と共に摘みました。私のチームは4人からなりオーストラリア人，スウェーデン人オーストリア人がいました。 |

## §4 商談通訳

### (1) メモ取り要約通訳

パッセージをサイトラして同時通訳の訳出パターンを検討して下さい。次にメモ化して下さい。

#### 労使関係　　　　　🎧2-12

**PM** Yesterday, I received a letter from one of our union executives in Manila. He expressed his concern about the labor relation conflicts and problems currently taking place in our Filipino subsidiary plant. It seems some of the workers are so upset about the working conditions and want to bring the union in to help resolve the dispute.
Before I report this matter to our Board, I'd like to get some advice from you. I'd like to come up with a solution so that we can avoid any industrial conflict. I realize that we may not be able to settle them well if we only look at this situation from our point of view. I wonder if taking the Japanese approach to problem solving, saving face and resolving the conflict privately will avoid a public scandal. We don't want to disrupt our business relation in any way.

**PR** まあ，一つの解決策は私がマニラに行き，彼等を説得してみるということです，部長の代わりに。私達フィリピン人の多くはこの種のトラブルは解決出来るはずだと考えます，労組を介入させる必要はないと思うのです。

**PM** I see. Then I'll talk to the Board about these complaints and grievances, this afternoon. We'll review the whole sitution together and come up with some possible solutions.

商談通訳

(2) センテンス逐次通訳

要約通訳が出来たらセンテンス逐次通訳に挑戦して下さい。

# Labor Relation

PM＝Personnel Manager（人事部長）
PR＝Production Manager（生産部長）

## 労使関係

**PM** 昨日，手紙がマニラの労働組合の役員から届きました。彼によると懸念があるそうです。それは労働紛争と問題についてで現在フィリピンの当社子会社でおこっていることです。
見たところ，労働者の何人かが労働条件について怒っており，労組を介入させてその紛争を解決するつもりだというのです。
この件を重役会に報告する前にあなたからアドバイスを頂きたいのです。解決策を見つけて労働争議を避けたいのです。
私の考えを申上げると，それらを解決出来ないこともありうると思うのです。この状況を私達の視点からのみ見るべきではないのです。
どうしたものでしょう，日本的アプローチで問題解決にあたり，面子をたてて，プライベートに紛争解決をして，スキャンダルを避けられるでしょうか。ビジネス関係を害したくないですね，ともかく。

**PR** Well, one possible solution is that I go to Manila myself and try to reason with them on behalf of our General Manager. Many of us Filipinos feel these kinds of troubles can be resolved without the involvement of labour unions.

**PM** なるほど。では，重役会にこれらの不満と苦情について話しておきましょう，今日の午後にでも。また全状況を一緒に見直して，何らかの解決策を打ち出しましょう。

## §5 メモ化リプロダクション

メモ化して下さい。メモをもとに聴衆に語りかけるように英語で発表して下さい。

# Japanese Garden 　　　2-13

There are three types of gardens in Japan. The first one is a flat garden such as a western style garden covered with flowers and plants. This type of garden is shaped in symmetry.
The second type is a hill garden. This hill garden is what we call a typical Japanese garden. The third one is a tea garden for tea ceremonies.

The garden is generally interpreted as a place set apart from the cultivation of flowers, fruit, vegetables and small plants of any kind. A garden is a place for meditation.

I would like to explain briefly the meaning of the various ornaments that are part of the garden, such as the pond, the small island within the pond, and the stone lanterns.
The pond stands for the sea, a lake, pond or river.
The bottom of the pond is usually made of clay.
The small island afloat in the middle of the pond signifies treasure island. It is shaped like a tortoise (turtle) and is decorated with pines.
The turtle is a symbol of longevity, the pine is a symbol of constancy.
The garden lantern which originated in old temples and shrines were first adopted as ornaments for the garden in the late 16th century. Since then, stone lanterns have become a vital part of the typical Japanese garden.

## §6　サイトラ原稿付き同時通訳

原稿を読み，訳出を工夫します（制限時間5分）。次にスピーチを聞きながら，なるべく同時通訳に聞こえるように訳出して下さい。

### Valentine's Day in Ireland

2-14
S. Moore

Whatever the origin of Valentine's Day, in Ireland people of every age celebrate it. Teenagers, single people and couples send cards to each other. If you send a card and you are single, you usually leave it unsigned so that person has to guess who sent it! A lot of guessing goes on especially if you are a student. Some "popular" people get quite a few cards.

Couples usually exchange cards. Some people go out for a romantic dinner and the man sometimes sends flowers (roses) and chocolates to his loved one. The flower shops are very busy on that day. The shops have a great selection of cards and presents that you can give to your darling, or someone you really like romantically on that day.

# Lesson 14

## §1 クイック・レスポンス

(1) ボキャビル

**演習方法**

英語と日本語の合成語を2秒以内で発音します。
次に日本語から英語，英語から日本語へ即時に変換して下さい。

## "Business" & In Search of Adventure 2

| | | |
|---|---|---|
| 1 | surplus | 黒字，余剰金 |
| 2 | deficit | 赤字 |
| 3 | interest | 利子 |
| 4 | dividend | 配当金 |
| 5 | annual income | 年収 |
| 6 | reimbursement | 払い戻し |
| 7 | debt | 負債 |
| 8 | expenditure | 支出 |
| 9 | finance | 財政 |
| 10 | be related to | 関係している |
| 11 | current | 現在の |
| 12 | unemployment | 失業 |
| 13 | denominator | 項，分母 |
| 14 | medical treatment | 医療 |
| 15 | prejudice | 偏見 |
| 16 | creed | 信条 |
| 17 | pending | 未決である |
| 18 | compromise | 妥協 |
| 19 | productivity | 生産性 |
| 20 | implement | 履行する，実行する |

(2) **数字**　英語に変換して下さい。

100億，315億，410億，515億，620億，1億，100億
190億，5000万，190億5000万，190億8000万，1190億，
1190億，7000万，7500万，1190億，7500万，1190億7500万

## §2　リテンションとリプロダクション

(1) **リテンション練習**
数回音読して暗唱して下さい。　　　　　　　　　🅞2-15

A  Could you clarify the requirements for this seminar?
B  Well you have 2 options. You can either write a research paper or give a presentation.
A  Excuse me that's the point I need to check. What kind of research paper did you have in mind?
B  A summary based on current research in our field.
   The topic should be related to current trends in software applications.

(2) **リプロダクション**
日本語文を読み，または聞き，即時に訳出して下さい。

A  このセミナーの必要条件を明確に言って下さいますか。
B  オプションは2つあります。リサーチ・ペーパーを書くかプレゼンテーションをすることです。
A  すみません。その点に関してチェックしたいのです。どの様なリサーチ・ペーパーをお考えですか？
B  サマリーです。私達の分野での最新のリサーチに基づいたものです。トピックはソフトウエア・アプリケーションにおいての現在のトレンドに関連するものでなければなりません。

## §3　区切り聞き

**演習方法**

初回は区切り聞きでリピーティング，二回目は該当部の日本語訳を音読して下さい。三回目からは自分の言葉で通訳して下さい。

# In Search of Adventure 2　　2-16

| | |
|---|---|
| Every morning | 毎朝 |
| we were woken up at 7 a.m., | 7時に起こされました。 |
| ready for our days' work | 仕事の準備をし， |
| to begin at 8 a.m. | 8時に始めました。 |
| If we worked hard | 一生懸命やれば |
| we could finish for the day | 終わることはできます |
| by about 12:30 p.m. | 12時半前に。 |
| Afternoons were usually spent | 午後は大抵 |
| swimming, playing soccer or reading. | 泳いだり，サッカーをしたり，読書をしました。 |
| I soon struck up | すぐに |
| numerous friendships | 色々な友達が |
| among the 50 other | 50もの |
| international volunteers | 国際ボランティアの中でできました。 |
| who came from all over the world, | 世界中からやってきた人々 |
| including Brazil, Holland, Norway, | それはブラジル，オランダ，ノルウェー， |
| the U.S.A. and South Africa. | アメリカ，南アフリカの人々です。 |
| Some had come on a kibbutz | ある人がキブツに来たのは |
| to escape from the northern European winter, | 北ヨーロッパの冬から逃れるため |
| others because of unemployment, | ある人の中には失業のため |

| | |
|---|---|
| a chance to study Hebrew for free, or like me | ヘブライ語をただで勉強するため または私の様に |
| for a spot of adventure. | 冒険のためにでした。 |
| The only common denominator amongst us was our need | 私たちの 共通項は |
| to use English to communicate with one another. | 英語を使うことでした，これで 意思の疎通を図ったのでした。 |
| On a kibbutz, | キブツでは |
| everything is basically free, | 全てが基本的には無料です。 |
| including food, accommodation, all sports facilities, | 食べ物，宿泊， 全スポーツ施設， |
| the use of cars | 車も |
| and medical treatment. | 医療もです。 |
| In the evenings | 夜は |
| we sometimes had parties | パーティーもあり |
| and international romances | 国際的なロマンスも |
| often flourished for these | よく芽生えました。こういう |
| young volunteers who were | 若いボランティアは寂しがったり |
| often lonely and homesick. | ホームシックになっていましたから。 |
| The lack of prejudice that developed among people | 偏見が無いということが 育まれていきました。 |
| from so many different nationalities, races and creeds | 色々な国籍や 人種や信条の人々の間で |
| was an inspiration | よいインスピレーションでした |
| and though it is not a perfect | 完全な制度ではないのですが |
| system, I would recommend it as an experience | キブツをお勧めしたいと思います。 |
| that shouldn't be missed. | のがしてはならない経験ですよ。 |

## §4　商談通訳

### (1) メモ取り要約通訳

パッセージをサイトラして同時通訳の訳出パターンを検討して下さい。次にメモ化して下さい。

### 協議事項のまとめ　　2-17

**MM** I think we have covered all the issues listed on today's agenda. Let's go over them just to make sure.
First, we have decided to assign the Minato team to the new project.
Second, with regard to the copyright problem, we'll have our lawyers look into the matter immediately.
Third, as for the new sales catalog, we've agreed on the prices, and the number of pages.
The lunch break issue is still pending, some sort of compromise has got to be negotiated with our union.

**TL** 私の考えは、有益な対策は意見の調査をしてから労組の役員に会うということです。
懸念は生産性が落ちるのではないかということです、もし新しい制度を実行したら。

**MM** I think it is a little premature to discuss this way further at the present time.
I'd like you to look this plan over and come up with some ideas so that we can settle this issue peacefully.
We cannot risk our reputation by having labor troubles.
Does anyone have anything to add?
Good, then we'll meet again next Tuesday.

(2) 逐次通訳

ウィスパリングがスムーズに出来たら逐次通訳に挑戦して下さい。

## **Summary**

MM＝Marketing Manager（マーケティング部長）
TL＝Team leader（チームリーダー）

MM　私の考えでは，本日の全協議事項をカバーしました。
もう一度，見直して確認しましょう。
第一に，港チームを新プロジェクトに割りあてることです。
第二，コピーライトの件は，当社弁護士を至急，調査にあたらせることです。
第三，新しいセールス・カタログに関しては価格とページ数についての合意ができました。
昼休みの件は未決で妥協案を当社労組と交渉します。


TL　I think it would be beneficial to take a poll before we start meeting with the union executives.
I'm afraid productivity will go down, if we implement this new system.

MM　考えますに，すこし時期尚早ですね，協議をこれ以上するのは現時点においては。
このプランを詳しく調べてなんらかのアイデアを出し，この件を平和的に解決しましょう。
当社の定評を危くすることはできません，労働問題を抱えることで。
どなたか，その他に補足することはありますか。
よろしい。では，来週の火曜に会いましょう。

## §5 メモ化リプロダクション

メモ化して下さい。メモをもとに聴衆に語りかけるように英語で発表して下さい。

## Marriage 　　2-18

I would like to talk about Japanese marriages.

Here in Japan the family, not the individual, has been for many centuries the social unit.

The new constitution of 1947 confirmed the right of an individual and the system has changed accordingly, but the traditional family idea still exists in the minds of many Japanese.

It is true that love marriages have been increasingly numerous, especially in urban areas. But many marriages are still arranged by friends of the involved families who act as go-betweens of each party. Usually a married couple become go-betweens as a pair, and make careful inquiries as to the suitability of the proposed match.

Before a definite settlement is reached, a rendez-vous of the prospective bride and groom is arranged. If both of them find their future spouse satisfactory, they decide to get married.
If the go-betweens are careful, they allow the couple a certain period for dating before they decide definitely. If it doesn't work out, it is the responsibility of the go-betweens to inform the rejected party diplomatically without hurting anyone's feeling.

We have an idea in Japan that marriage is the beginning of love and not the result of it.

## §6　簡単な同時通訳

初見で同時通訳して下さい。

予備知識：最近，福島の白河に研修施設の British Hills を開設した K 校の校長が，関係者の集まりで，この施設についてスピーチをしました。

### A Cultural Experience　2-19

| | |
|---|---|
| Ladies and gentlemen, | ご列席の皆さん |
| Our institute has recently | 当学院は最近 |
| obtained the services of | サービスを受けられます |
| "British Hills" in Shirakawa. | 白河ブリティッシュ・ヒルズの |
| The center was set up | センターが設立されました |
| with a view to providing | 目的は |
| an authentic cultural setting | 本物の文化的セッティングを提供し |
| in which the general public | その中で一般の人が |
| could attend seminars | セミナーに参加でき |
| mainly using English as the | 主に英語を使用しながら |
| medium of communication. | コミュニケーションを図ることです。 |
| It has long been known that | 昔からよく知られていますように |
| environment is an important factor | 環境が重要です |
| in language studies. | 語学の勉強をするには。 |
| This center offers a perspective | 当センターが提供する視点は |
| into Anglo-Japanese relations. | 英日関係の全体を見渡して下さい。 |
| I do hope that | 願うのは |
| you will take advantage of | 皆様にご利用いただくことです。 |
| the facilities and services | 施設とサービスが |
| that are available | ご提供できますので |
| in our organisation. | 当組織では。 |

# Lesson 15

## §1 クイック・レスポンス

(1) ボキャビル

**演習方法**

英語と日本語の合成語を2秒以内で発音します。
次に日本語から英語，英語から日本語へ即時変換して下さい。

## Business & Out of Africa 1

| | | |
|---|---|---|
| 1 | strategy | 戦略 |
| 2 | tactics | 作戦 |
| 3 | effective | 効果的 |
| 4 | efficient | 能率的 |
| 5 | risky | 危険 |
| 6 | estimation | 見積り |
| 7 | evaluation | 評価 |
| 8 | mortgage | 担保 |
| 9 | settle accounts | 勘定を支払う |
| 10 | pay damages | 損害賠償を支払う |
| 11 | state | 状態 |
| 12 | ferment | 動揺，発酵 |
| 13 | struggle(d) to | 苦労をして〜する，もがく |
| 14 | identity | アイデンティティ，自己確立 |
| 15 | luxuriance | 華美 |
| 16 | vigour | 活力 |
| 17 | excessiveness | 極端さ |
| 18 | equatorial | 赤道下の |
| 19 | tropical thunderstorm | 熱帯雷雨 |
| 20 | valid | 妥当な，有効な |

(2) **数字**　英語に即時変換して下さい。

200億，35億，401億，1億7500万，620億，200万，
33万，15万，2455万，3333万，18万9000，9億，
6500万年前，600年前，60億人，1億2000万人

## §2　リテンションとリプロダクション

(1) **リテンション練習**

数回音読して暗唱して下さい。　　　　　　　　2-20

A  Have you had a chance to go over our proposal?
B  Yes, I have. Can I ask you some questions about it?
A  Certainly.
B  You talked about changes in our systems. It isn't clear what kind of changes are meant.
A  Those are explained in Section 3.
B  I see. Now I understand.

(2) **リプロダクション練習**

日本語文を読み，または聞き，即時に訳出して下さい。

A  私どもの提案をご覧いただけましたか。
B  はい，あれに関して幾つか質問がありますがいいですか。
A  もちろんです。
B  制度上の変革についての話がありましたね。それが明確では無いのですが，どの様な変革ですか。
A  それらはセクション3に説明してあります。
B  なるほど，わかりました。

## §3　区切り聞き

**演習方法**

初回は区切り聞きでリピーティング，二回目は該当部の日本語訳を音読，三回目からはリテインしながら自分の言葉で通訳して下さい。

# Out of Africa 1

2-21　A. Goodman

| | |
|---|---|
| Although I began my teaching career in Scotland and the Western Pacific, | 私が教師として教え始めたのはスコットランドと西太平洋でしたが |
| it was really in West Africa | 本当は西アフリカでした |
| that I first started to think about | 私が |
| how people learn a new language and how we can create | 人々が新しい言語を習う方法と |
| ideal conditions for this learning. | それに対しての理想的な状況をつくるこを考え始めたのは。 |
| I would like to share | |
| these early experiences with you because I think | 初期の経験をお話しします。それは |
| you will find something there | それにより何か |
| to help you become | 助けになるものを見つけ |
| more fluent speakers | より言語が流暢に話せる |
| of other languages, whatever | 人になるためです。 |
| those languages may be. | 言語が何語であろうとも。 |
| West Africa in the old days | 昔の西アフリカは |
| was an exciting place to be in. | すごく面白いところでした |
| Perhaps it lacked the beauty of East Africa, | 多分東アフリカの美しさはなかったかもしれませんが |
| but its human landscape was much richer. | 人的背景はより豊富でした。 |
| I am sure it still retains | きっとまだ残っているはずです |

| | |
|---|---|
| its charm and cultural richness. | その魅力と豊かな文化は。 |
| When I was there | 私がそこにいたとき |
| the whole area | 全地域が |
| was in a state of ferment. | 政治的に動揺していました |
| All kinds of forces were at work | 全ての勢力が活動しており |
| as Africans struggled | アフリカ人が苦労して |
| to find a new identity | 新しい自己確立の道を探し |
| and create a new society | 新しい社会を造ろうとして |
| for themselves | いました |
| after decades of colonial rule. | 何十年もの植民地支配の後で。 |
| It was strange | 不思議なのは |
| that they should have used | 彼等は |
| the old colonial languages, | 古い植民地時代の言語を |
| English and French, to express | 英語とフランス語を使っていた |
| their thoughts and feelings, | のです |
| but they did. | 考えや感情の表現に。 |
| The students in the Nigerian | ナイジェリア大学の学生は |
| university where I taught | そこで私はフランス語を教えていた |
| French loved language. | のですが，言語が大好きでした。 |
| They loved words, powerful words to | 彼等が好んだのは強力な感情を |
| express powerful feelings. | 表す強力な言葉です。 |
| There was a luxuriance, a vigour, an excessiveness | 華美，活力 極端さが |
| in their speech and writing | スピーチや著述にあり |
| that reminded you | それで思い出したのが |
| of the equatorial forest | 赤道下の森林や |
| and the tropical thunderstorm. | 熱帯雷雨です。 |
| The students were drunk with words. | 学生達は言葉に酔っていました。 |

## §4 メモ取り要約通訳

パッセージをサイトラして同時通訳の訳出パターンを検討して下さい。次にパラグラフごとに聞きながらメモを取って要約通訳し，最後にウィスパリング通訳練習をして下さい。

### 討議 💿2-22

**MM** 新型モデルのマーケティング戦略を部内で話し合ってみました。
そして，うちの部ではテレビと雑誌の両方で宣伝するべきだと考えています。

**CM** I'm afraid I don't agree with you. Last autumn we sponsored a women's symposium, and when that event was featured on mass media we had a marked increase in product sales. We found that to be a very successful marketing strategy.

**MM** そうでしたね。でも，今年は違ったアプローチで買い物客の注意を引きたいと思います。人はイメージに基づいて物を買いますからね。私どもの目標はイメージ・アップをすることなのです。

**CM** I understand your argument. However TV commercials are more expensive than sponsoring forums.

**MM** はい，それはそうですが，今回はキャンペーンを拡大し，大衆に関心を持たせられますから，やってみる価値はあると思います。
ですから，テレビ・コマーシャルを活用することによりもっと若者達が当社の製品を買うようになるかもしれません。

**CM** I see your point, but I still feel commercials, in the end, would be less lucrative.

**MM** そうかもしれません。しかし，私どものマーケット・リサーチによると，当社製品のようなより豪華なものへの需要が高まってきています。

**CM** You make a valid point. Therefore before we make any final decision, I think it would be a good idea to do some cost comparative research.

ウィスパリングが出来たら逐次通訳に挑戦して下さい。

## Discussion

MM＝Marketing Manager　　CM＝Commercial Manager
　（マーケティング担当部長）　　（営業部長）

**MM** We've discussed the marketing strategy for the new models in our section, and we think we should advertise both on TV and in magazines.

**CM** それには賛成出来かねます。去年の秋に女性達のシンポジウムを後援したとき，そのイベントがマスメディアに取り上げられて製品の売り上げが著しく伸びましたね。あれは非常にうまいマーケティング戦略だったと思っています。

**MM** I remember that, but this year we want to impress consumers by taking a different approach. People buy things based on image. Our goal is to promote those images.

**CM** あなたのおっしゃることはわかります。しかし，テレビ・コマーシャルはフォーラムの後援よりも高額です。

**MM** Yes, that's a given ; But this time we should expand our campaign and we think with the huge audience we will reach, it's worth trying. We are sure of our products' superior quality, so by utilizing television by way of commercials more young people would be inclined to buy our products.

**CM** お話のポイントは理解出来ますが，コマーシャルでは結局，儲からないという気がするのです。

**MM** It's true we could lose, but according to our market research there's a growing demand for more luxurious items like ours.

**CM** ごもっともです。したがいまして，最終決定をする前に，価格の比較検討をしてみるのがよいと思われます。

## §5  通訳基本練習

### (1)  日英通訳練習

#### 着物と帯

1  日本人女性の多くが公式の場で着物を着ます。
2  完全な正式の着物は二，三枚の内側に着る物と美しい外側の着物からなっています。
3  普通着物は必要以上に長くなっています。
4  ですから着る人が長さを調節します。
5  帯と呼ばれるサッシュがそれら全てをうまくまとめておきます。
6  女性用の帯は約2メートルあります。
7  それは背中に締めます。
8  正式な場合は既婚の女性は黒い着物を着ます。
9  黒い着物は家紋が袂と背に付いています。
10  独身女性はカラフルな振り袖を着ます。

### (2)  ワン・センテンス遅れ通訳の練習

#### 着物と帯

　先日，たまたま着物を着た外国人女性を見ました。それはある東京の一流ホテルのロビーでした。私はそれを見て驚きました。彼女は安い観光客のお土産用の着物を着ていたのです。そして帯は前で結んでありました。その場にはそぐわない感じでした。ロビーにいた人は皆あきれたまなざしで彼女を見ました。

　歌舞伎や歴史劇を見るとき，着物を着て帯をお腹の上に結んでいる人々が舞台の上に見えるかもしれません。それは良いのです。俳優や女優ですから。昔，日本人女性の階級は帯のスタイルで見分けられました。帯を前で結んでいた人達はまともな女性とは見なされませんでした。もし，着物を着て人前に出る場合は，正しい着付を習うのがいいでしょう。

## Kimono and Obi      2-23

1. Many Japanese women wear kimono on formal occasions.
2. The full formal kimono consists of a few layers of inner kimono and a beautiful outside kimono.
3. Usually a kimono is longer than necessary.
4. So the wearer adjusts the length.
5. A sash called an obi holds all of these in place.
6. The obi for a woman is about 2 meters in length.
7. It is tied on the back.
8. In formal occasions, married women wear a black kimono.
9. The black kimono is supposed to have the crests of her family on the sleeves and the back.
10. Single girls wear colorful kimono with long sleeves.

## Kimono and Obi      2-24

The other day I happened to see a foreign lady wearing a kimono.
It was in a lobby of a prestigious hotel in Tokyo. I was shocked at the sight. What she had on was the type of inexpensive souvenir kimono for tourists. And she had tied her obi in front. It looked out of place. Everybody in the lobby was giving rather a dirty look at her.

If you go to see Kabuki or a historical play, you may see people in kimono with their obi tied on the stomach on stage. It's OK because they are actors or actresses. In olden days Japanese women's classes were differentiated by obi styles. Those who used to tie obis in front were not regarded as decent women. So if you want to wear a kimono in public, it's a good idea to learn to put it on properly.

# Lesson 16

## §1 クイック・レスポンス

(1) ボキャビル

**演習方法**

英語と日本語の合成語を2秒以内で発音します。
次に日本語から英語，英語から日本語へ即時変換して下さい。

## Business & Out of Africa 2

| | | |
|---|---|---|
| 1 | found | 創立する |
| 2 | merger | 合併 |
| 3 | acquisition | 買収 |
| 4 | optical devices | 光学機器 |
| 5 | current situation | 現在の状況 |
| 6 | microscope(s) | 顕微鏡 |
| 7 | photographic equipment | 写真機 |
| 8 | allowance | 手当 |
| 9 | benefit(s) | 給付金 |
| 10 | personnel | 人事 |
| 11 | seniority system | 年功序列制 |
| 12 | canteen | 売店 |
| 13 | in the red | 赤字で |
| 14 | adolescent | 青春期，思春期 |
| 15 | subversive | 危険分子 |
| 16 | cruel tyrant | 残忍な圧制者 |
| 17 | man of letters | 文学者，著述者 |
| 18 | literary genius | 文学の天才 |
| 19 | disapprove | 不可とする |
| 20 | rollick | はしゃぎ回る |

(2) **数字** 英語に変換して下さい。

3200億, 6635億, 1001億, 2500万, 620億, 620億2500万,
4200億, 6035億, 1000億, 2600万, 622億, 621億2500万

## §2 リテンションとリプロダクション

(1) **リテンション練習**
数回音読して暗唱して下さい。　　　　　　　　2-25

A The company canteen has been in the red for the last 6 months.
B That's due to the rising costs. Anyway, at this rate, I'm afraid we are going to have to close the canteen in the near future.
A Why not try re-examining the supplier we buy from?
B The matter is not that simple, but it is worth a try.
A All the workers are quite concerned whether the canteen can be kept open or not.

(2) **リプロダクション**
日本語文を読み，または聞き，即時に訳出して下さい。

A 社内の売店がもう半年間赤字を出しています。
B 諸物価上昇のためです。とにかくこの率でいくと，将来的には売店を閉鎖しなければならなくなります。
A 納入業者を再検討してみたらどうでしょう。
B そんなに簡単な問題ではないでしょうが，やってみる価値はありますね。
A 従業員全員が心配していますのは，売店をそのままにしておけるかどうかです。

## §3 区切り聞き

**演習方法**

初回は区切り聞きでリピーティング,二回目は該当部の日本語訳を音読,三回目からはリテインしながら自分の言葉で通訳して下さい。

# Out of Africa 2　🄯2-26

| | |
|---|---|
| I studied the plays of Wole Soyinka | 私はウォーレ・ソインカの劇を研究し |
| and learned a lot from him. | 彼から色々学びました。 |
| He later won the Nobel prize for literature, | 彼は後にノーベル賞を<br>文学で受賞しました |
| but when I was in Nigeria, | 私がナイジェリアにいた当時 |
| he was in jail | 彼は監獄にいました |
| for political activism. | 政治活動のためにです。 |
| His enemies called him a "subversive". | 彼の政敵は彼を危険分子と呼びました。 |
| His worst enemy was later cut up into little pieces by the people. | 彼の最悪の政敵は後に<br>人々に切りきざまれました |
| I didn't feel the least bit sorry for that cruel tyrant. | 私はその残忍な圧政者がかわいそうだとは思いませんでした。 |
| But I did feel sorry for Wole Soyinka. | でもウォーレ・ソインカは気の毒だと思いました。 |
| 　While in West Africa, I also studied the works of the Senegalese poet, | 西アフリカにいるあいだ<br>私は研究しました<br>セネガルの詩人のセンゴールの作品を, |
| Senghor who also deserved the Nobel prize. | 彼もまたノーベル賞に値する人でした。 |
| I can't think why | どうして |
| the writings of these<br>great African men of letters | 偉大なアフリカの文学者達の作品は |

| | |
|---|---|
| are so little studied in Japan. | 日本で研究されないのでしょうか。 |
| Japanese scholars and critics | 日本の学者や批評家達は |
| seem to disapprove of anything | 評価をしないようです |
| that comes out of Africa, | アフリカのものに対しては |
| but how can you look down | でも見下すことは出来ません |
| on pure literary genius? | 真に文学の天才を。 |
| I am sure that many an | きっと多くの |
| African Shakespeare has lived | アフリカ人シェークスピアが, |
| his life unnoticed by the | 気付かれることなく生き, |
| critics and the reading public. | 批評家や大衆の読書家に知られなかったことでしょう。 |
| I found Africans to be | アフリカ人は |
| linguistic geniuses and | 言語の天才達で |
| I wondered why this was so. | その理由が何でか考えました。 |
| Our students became more | 学生が |
| fluent than their teachers! | 先生達よりも流暢になったのです。 |
| At first I thought | まず考えられたのは |
| it had something to do | きっと |
| with their culture | 文化に関係しているのだろう |
| or the multilingual nature | 多言語 |
| of tribal society. | 部族社会ですから。 |
| You know, once you learn a | ご存じのように |
| second language as a child, | 子供の時に二つ目の言語を学ぶと |
| your third comes more easily. | 三つ目はもっと簡単になります。 |
| But this was not the real reason. | でもこれが本当の理由ではありませんでした。 |
| The professor and the teachers, | 教授や教員達は |
| however, were convinced | 確信していました。 |
| that it was the new teaching method | 新しい教授法 |
| we had imported from France | フランスから導入したものが |
| that produced the miracle. | 奇跡的成果を生み出したことを。 |

## §4　商談通訳

即時変換して下さい。

### 合弁事業の検討

2-27

**GM:** さて，新合弁事業計画の事前報告を読まれましたね。あの，オーストラリアに生化学製品の研究センターをつくるというものです。どう思われますか。

**PM:** As I see it, there seem to be some problems with the project. One being that it is a time-consuming project; Also we have to keep the systems 100% environmentally friendly, which will cost too much for our stock-holders to be happy. I'm afraid some of the technicians won't be very enthusiastic, either.

**GM:** 問題は幾つかありますが，こちらの人達は大部分が違った意見を持つでしょうね。多角的なプロジェクトを行う可能性が出てくることになるのですから。
例えば，大規模な水栽工場を建てて野菜や果物を生産することも可能ですね。

**PM:** That's an interesting approach, if there is more than a research center, we can create more jobs for the local people, as well.

**GM:** はい，これなら，うちの重役会の目的に適うかもしれませんね。

## A joint venture consideration

GM : General Manger　　　　PM : Production Manager
　　（ジェネラル・マネージャー）　　（生産部長）

**GM:** Well, you've read the preliminary report about the new joint venture project to set up a research center of bio-chemical products in Australia. What do you think of it?

**PM:** 私が見たところでは，この計画には幾つか問題点があります。
一つは，時間がかかることです。それに，設備を全て環境にやさしくしなければなりません。これは，金が掛かり過ぎて株主が喜びませんね。それに，技術者のうちの何人かがあまり乗り気にならないと思いますね。

**GM:** Although we do have some problems here, most of our people would have different opinions since there will be more possibilities for us to carry out diversified projects. One possibility, for instance, is that we can have a large scale hydro-ponic plant to produce vegetables and fruits.

**PM:** 面白いアプローチですね。もし研究センター以上のものなら，付近の住民に職を提供することも出来ますね。

**GM:** Good. This may fit in with our Board's objectives.

## §5　通訳基本練習

### (1)　通訳ガイド練習

#### 皇居前広場

1　元は皇居は江戸城と呼ばれていました。
2　この城は1457年に太田道灌により建てられました。
3　1590年に徳川家康に占拠されました。
4　家康は城を多大の時間をかけ拡張しました。
5　1868年に明治天皇は京都から江戸城に移りました。
6　明治維新以降皇族は東京に住んでいます。
7　皇居前広場に二つの橋があります。
8　それらは二重橋，英語ではダブル・ブリッジと呼ばれています。
9　それらが宮殿への正門を形成しています。
10　新宮殿は1967年に完成しました。

### (2)　ワン・センテンス遅れ訳

#### 皇居

　石垣とお堀が見えたら，それは皇居の近くです。そこに天皇が住んでいます。昔は京都が1000年間日本の首都でした。ですから，京都にはまだ古い御所があります。

　現皇居では年に二回一般参賀があります。1月2日と天皇誕生日です。

　もし，石垣の中を訪ねてみたいのなら，東御苑を見学できます。そこで見られるのは伝統的な庭園で，小堀遠州によって造形されたものです。もし，天皇にお会いになりたいのなら，ボランティア・ワーカーとして働いて下さい。四日働いた後で天皇に会うことができます。

　ちなみに，天皇は立憲君主です。君臨しますが，統治はしません。

## Imperial Palace Plaza  🔊 2-28

1 Originally, the Imperial Palace was called Edo Castle.
2 The castle was built in 1457 by Dokan Ota.
3 In 1590 the castle was seized by Ieyasu Tokugawa.
4 Ieyasu spent a great deal of time in expanding the castle.
5 In 1868 Emperor Meiji moved into Edo castle from Kyoto.
6 Since the Meiji Restoration the Imperial family has been living in Tokyo.
7 In the Imperial Palace Plaza, you see two bridges.
8 They are called Nijubashi or Double Bridges, in English.
9 They form the main entrance to the Palace.
10 The New Palace was completed in 1967.

## Imperial Palace  🔊 2-29

When you see stone walls and moats, you are near the Imperial Palace. That's where our Emperor lives.

In the past Kyoto used be the capital of Japan for 1000 years. So there is still the old palace in Kyoto.

The present Palace is opened to the public twice a year, on January 2nd and the Emperor's birthday.

If you want to go inside the stone walls, you can visit East garden. You can see a traditional garden laid out by Enshu Kobori. If you want to meet our Emperor, please work as a volunteer worker. After 4 days of work, you can see him face to face.

By the way, our Emperor is a constitutional monarch.
He reigns, but does not rule.

# Lesson 17

## §1 クイック・レスポンス

(1) ボキャビル

**演習方法**

英語と日本語の合成語を2秒以内で発音します。
次に日本語から英語，英語から日本語へ即時変換して下さい。

## Business & Out of Africa 3

| | | |
|---|---|---|
| 1 | manufacturing industry | 製造業 |
| 2 | distribution industry | 流通業 |
| 3 | petrochemical industry | 石油化学工業 |
| 4 | automobile industry | 自動車産業 |
| 5 | information industry | 情報産業 |
| 6 | service industry | サービス業 |
| 7 | leisure industry | レジャー産業 |
| 8 | steel industry | 鉄鋼業 |
| 9 | shipbuilding industry | 造船業 |
| 10 | precision industry | 精密産業 |
| 11 | advertising | 広告業 |
| 12 | oil business | 石油産業 |
| 13 | develop new lines | 新しいラインを開発する |
| 14 | witchery | 妖術 |
| 15 | marvellous | 驚くべき |
| 16 | sole | 唯一の |
| 17 | means of communicating | 通信する手段 |
| 18 | interact | 対話する |
| 19 | informant(s) | 報告者 |
| 20 | share | 分け合う |

Lesson 17　149

(2) **数字**　英語に変換して下さい。

6億, 5,000万, 9億, 9億5,000万, 30万, 10億, 20億, 200億, 300億, 350億, 4000億, 3000億, 5500億

## §2　リテンションとリプロダクション

(1) **リテンション練習**

数回音読して暗唱して下さい。　　　　　　　　　　　2-30

A　I want to know if you can help us get statistics on hot drinks sales in the Pacific region.
B　Well, certainly, but could you give us some more details as we may be able to provide better service when we know the purpose of the research.
A　Oh, yes. My name is Kevin Sullivan. I'm the marketing manager of East West Chemicals. We are thinking of developing new lines for the Pacific region. We want to see if we can move into this field of business.

(2) **リプロダクション練習**

日本語文を読み，または聞き，即時に訳出して下さい。

A　太平洋地域でのホット・ドリンク売上高の統計を入手していただけますか。
B　はい，勿論ですが，もう少し詳細をお知らせ願えますか。
　　御社のリサーチの目的がわかると，より良いサービスをご提供出来るかもしれませんので。
A　はい，わたしはケビン・サリヴァンで東西化学のマーケティング部長です。太平洋地域用の製品を開発しようと思っています。
　　この分野のビジネスに参入できるかを知りたいのです。

## §3　区切り聞き

### 演習方法

初回は区切り聞きでリピーティング，二回目は該当部の日本語訳を音読します。最後に自分の言葉で通訳して下さい。

## Out of Africa 3　　🄯2-31

| | |
|---|---|
| In France, LL's had reached an advanced stage of development and our university set up an LL. | フランスではLLが発展進歩をとげ私達の大学はLLを設置しました。 |
| It was the first such lab in black Africa | それはアフリカの黒人の国では初めてのもので， |
| and we were very proud of it. | 私たちの自慢でした。 |
| Yet the students themselves did not spend so much time in the lab and I wondered | しかし，学生達はあまり時間をLLに費やさず，私は不思議に思いました， |
| by what magic and witchery they became so marvellously fluent in only a few months. | どの様な魔法で彼等が驚くほどの流暢さを二，三か月で身に付けたのかと。 |
| After a year they were almost bilingual. | 一年して彼等はほとんどバイリンガルになっていました。 |
| They didn't learn very much in the LL | 彼等はあまりLLでは学ばず |
| and they probably learned even less in the classroom, | 多分教室ではそれ以下でした |
| so how did they come by their new fluency? | どうやって流暢になったのでしょう？ |
| The secret lay in their rich social interactions | 秘密は豊富に社交が相互にあったからです。 |

| | |
|---|---|
| using the new language | 新しい言語を使って |
| as the sole means of communicating with one another. | それのみを意思伝達の手段にしたのです。 |
| At breaktime, at parties, | 休み時間に，パーティーに， |
| on trips, in the dormitories, | 旅行に，寮に |
| the seniors who knew most | 3年生で良く知っている人達は |
| would interact with the juniors | 2年生と交流し |
| who in turn would interact | 2年生は |
| with the freshmen. | 新入生と交流したのです。 |
| The students were each others' | 学生達自身が |
| informants. | 情報を提供しあったのです |
| When the Seniors came back | 3年生が |
| from their study tour in | 修学旅行で行った |
| Senegal or in the Ivory Coast, | セネガルや象牙海岸から戻った時 |
| they would share | 披露したのです |
| their new knowledge | 新しい知識を |
| with the younger students | 年下の学生に |
| who had had to stay (at) home. | 留守番役の下級生に。 |
| This is a lesson that Africans | このレッスンはつまり |
| can teach us 〜 the value of | アフリカ人達が教えてくれるのは |
| community learning. | 生活共同体での学習の大切さです。 |
| Learning does not stop | 学習は終わりません |
| when the classroom bell rings, | 終業のベルが鳴ったとしても |
| but continues on into your | 続きます |
| club meetings, your parties, | クラブ活動やパーティーや |
| your practising of speeches | スピーチの練習や |
| and your study trips. | 修学旅行にも。 |
| So keep your lips moving! | だから，唇を動かし続けること。 |
| Good luck! | グッド・ラック！ |

## §4　商談通訳

### (1)　メモ取り要約通訳

パッセージをサイトラして同時通訳の訳出パターンを検討して下さい。次にパラグラフごとに聞きながらメモを取って要約通訳し，最後にウィスパリング通訳練習をして下さい。

**価格交渉**　　2-32

**PM**　Now we would like to continue discussion on the price and terms of payment. Your quotation is too high for us and we are not sure we will be able to persuade our dealers to accept these price offerings. We hope you give us more acceptable terms for payment, too.

**SM**　では，御社の希望価格と支払い条件をお聞かせ下さい。

**PM**　We'd like a 35% discount and an evenly split payment over 5 years.

**SM**　残念なのですが私どもが提供出来る最大割引は 25％です。しかし，支払いについては譲歩できます。

**PM**　Without discount, we will be unable to achieve our sales volumes. You know our current position is to put market share above profit, at least in the coming few years. So we have to ask you to keep your margin as low as you can. Otherwise, we won't be flexible in marketing these products.

**SM**　御社の申し込み条件は非常に難しいものです。私どもは社内で協議しなければなりません。ここで，一時中断して一か月以内にまた会うということにしましょうか。

(2) 逐次通訳
ウィスパリングがスムーズに出来たら逐次通訳に挑戦して下さい。

# Price negotiation

PM＝Production manager　　SM＝Sales manager
　　（生産部長）　　　　　　　　（販売部長）

**PM** さて，引き続き価格と支払い条件の協議をしたいと思います。
御社の価格は高すぎて私どものディーラーの方々がこれらの価格提供で納得してくれるか確信がもてません。御社がもっと受け入れやすい支払い条件を提示してくださることを願っています。

**SM** Then tell us the prices and the terms you want.

**PM** 35％引きで5年間の定額支払いがよろしいのですが。

**SM** I'm afraid the largest discount we can give you is 25% but we can concede about the payment.

**PM** 割引なしでは売り上げ数が達成出来ません。
ご存じのように，私どもは現在利益よりも市場占有率を優先しております。少なくともこの二，三年はこの体制でやっていく次第です。ですから，御社の利ざやを出来るだけ低くして頂くようお願いしたいのです。さもなければ，これらの製品を販売するための柔軟性がなくなってしまうのです。

**SM** Your proposal is very hard. We have to discuss it on our side. Can we stop here and come back within one month?

# §5 通訳基本練習

## (1) 通訳ガイド

### 浅草

1　1360年ほど前に三人の漁師が小さい観音像を隅田川で発見しました。
2　彼等は簡単な礼拝堂をその像のために建てました。
3　浅草観音は東京で一番古い寺です。
4　本堂は1958年に再建されたものです。
5　寺は聖観音宗に属しています。
6　卍のマークはナチのマークとは関係ありません。
7　それらのマークはドイツのものよりずっと古いものです。
8　仏教ではそれらは恩恵と精神的幸福のシンボルです。
9　日本では卍は仏教を表すシンボルです。
10　五重塔は五つの自然の要素を表しています。すなわち，地，火，水，風，空です。

## (2) ワンセンテンス遅れ訳

### 浅草

　浅草にはたくさんのお祭りや年中行事があります。一番有名なのは三社祭りです。神道のお祭りです。主なアトラクションは100基以上のお御輿が地域を清めるために担がれることです。

　夏は大勢の人達が花火を見に来ます。15,000発以上もの花火が隅田川上空に打ち上げられます。

　サンバ・カーニバルは西洋風のお祭りです。毎年ブラジル人達がリオデ・ジャネイロから招かれ東京人と一緒に踊ります。

　ホオズキ市と羽子板市は私の好きな市です。ホオズキはグランド・チェリーで市とはフェアーのことです。羽子板市では装飾の付いた羽子板と羽を売っています。

## Asakusa  🄔2-33

1   About 1360 years ago three fishermen found a small image of Kannon on the Sumida River.
2   They built a simple place of worship for the image.
3   Asakusa Kannon Temple is the oldest temple in Tokyo.
4   The main hall was rebuilt in 1958.
5   The temple belongs to the Sho Kannon sect.
6   The swastika symbols have nothing to do with the Nazi mark.
7   They are much older than the German ones.
8   In Buddhism they are the symbols of blessing and spiritual happiness.
9   In Japan the swastika is a symbol to represent Buddhism.
10  Five-storied pagodas represent the five natural elements; ground, fire, water, wind and sky.

## Asakusa  🄔2-34

In Asakusa there are so many festivals and annual events. The most famous festival is the Sanja Matsuri. It's a Shinto festival. The main attraction of this festival is that over 100 portable shrines are carried to purify the area.

In summer a lot of people come to see fireworks. More than 15,000 fireworks are launched over the Sumida River.
The Samba carnival is a western type festival. Each year some Brazilians are invited to come from Rio de Janeiro to dance with Tokyoites.

Hohzuki Ichi and Hagoita ichi are my favorite fairs. Hohzuki means ground cherries and ich means a fair. Hagoita ichi is where they sell decorated battledore and shuttlecocks.

# Lesson 18

## §1 クイック・レスポンス

(1) ボキャビル

**演習方法**

英語と日本語の合成語を2秒以内で発音します。
次に日本語から英語, 英語から日本語へ即時に変換して下さい。

## Business & Calcutta 1

| | | |
|---|---|---|
| 1 | monopoly | 独占 |
| 2 | R & D | 研究・開発 |
| 3 | memorandum | 覚え書き |
| 4 | draft | 為替手形, 草稿 |
| 5 | agreement | 契約 |
| 6 | inventory | 商品目録 |
| 7 | overhead | 一般諸経費 |
| 8 | account | 取引先 |
| 9 | bidding | 入札 |
| 10 | premises | 不動産, 敷地 |
| 11 | come to a conclusion | 結論に達する |
| 12 | pay off | 採算がとれる |
| 13 | faded | 色あせた |
| 14 | monks | 僧 |
| 15 | nuns | 尼僧 |
| 16 | devotees | 信者 |
| 17 | seeking knowledge | 知識をもとめ |
| 18 | bliss | 無上の幸福 |
| 19 | liberation | 解放 |
| 20 | overcome | 打ち勝つ |

(2) **数字** 英語に変換して下さい。

2億＋4億＝6億, 15億＋10億＝25億, 20億－9億＝11億,
1000万×91＝9億1000万, 6000万×11＝6億6000万,
2500万－10万＝2490万, 105万＋105万＝210万,
200億－160億＝40億, 400万÷4＝100万,
$2^2$ (2 squared),
$2^5$ (2 raised to the 5th power),
$3^3$ (3 cubed),
2：2＝4：4 (2 to 2 equals 4 to 4.)

## §2 リテンションとリプロダクション

(1) **リテンション練習**
    数回音読して暗唱して下さい。　　　　　2-35

A  I hear our company has bought some premises in Hawaii.
B  Right. It was about 3 days ago. It was a big investment. Our board had considered it for quite a while. And they came to the conclusion that it would pay off.
A  What are they like?
B  I only saw some pictures, but they are nice.

(2) **リプロダクション練習**
    日本語文を読み、または聞き、即時に訳出して下さい。

A  うちの会社はハワイに不動産を買ったそうですね。
B  ええ、そうです。三日ほど前です。大型投資でした。
    重役会は相当の間考慮しました。それで採算がとれるという結論に達したのです。
A  どの様なものなのですか?
B  写真を何枚か見ただけなのですが、素敵ですよ。

## §3 区切り聞き

**演習方法**

初回は区切り聞きでリピーティング，二回目は該当部の日本語訳を音読して下さい。最後は自分の言葉で通訳して下さい。

### Calcutta 1

2-36
H. Bartelen

| | |
|---|---|
| "Chai, chai, chai." | 『チャイ，チャイ，チャイ』 |
| The calls of the tea sellers | お茶売りの声が |
| were ringing throughout the air. | 響き渡っていました。 |
| I was at the train station | 私は |
| in Calcutta, India. | インドのカルカッタ駅にいました。 |
| My friend, Ananda, | 友人のアーナンダは |
| in his faded pink shirt, | 色あせたピンクのシャツを着て |
| stood in front of me. | 私の前に立っていました。 |
| We had become friends | 友達になったのは |
| at the yoga center | ヨガセンターです。 |
| where we had met. | そこで出会いました。 |
| The yoga center, or ashram | センターは |
| as it was called; | アシュラムと呼ばれ |
| was full of orange-robed monks | オレンジ色の衣を着た僧や |
| and nuns, devotees and travelers | 尼僧や信者や旅行者でいっぱいで |
| seeking knowledge and waiting | した。彼等は知識を求め |
| to hear the guru's words | 待っていました。グールーの無上の |
| of bliss and liberation. | 幸福と解放の言葉を聞くのを。 |
| The guru's words, however, | グールーの言葉は |
| seemed so distant | 遠くに行ってしまったようです。 |
| as the sounds of the station | |
| overcame my senses. | 駅の物音に圧倒されました。 |
| Ananda handed me | アーナンダは |
| some small, green bananas | 小さい緑のバナナをくれ |

| | |
|---|---|
| and with an embrace, | 抱擁して |
| wished me good-bye. | さよならを言いました。 |
| "Don't forget to write | 『手紙と |
| and don't forget about your meditation." | 瞑想を忘れるなよ。』 |
| I smiled back and said, "Namaskar" | 私は頬笑んでナマスカルとインド流 |
| the Indian good-bye. | の『さよなら』を言いました。 |
| The tea sellers were close by | お茶売りは近くにおり |
| and the aroma of hot tea and milk mingled with the dirt and the dust. | ホットティとミルクの香りが汚れとほこりに混じっていました。 |
| Just as I was about to get on the train, | 汽車に乗ろうとしたとき |
| I saw a blind girl, | 目の不自由な少女が |
| supported by the arms of her mother, approaching strangers for money. | 自分の母親に支えられ物乞いにやって来るのを見ました。 |
| Oh Calcutta, so poor, so desperate and yet so animated. | カルカッタよ，何と貧しく絶望的でその反面活気があることか。 |
| My week in Calcutta was over. | カルカッタでの一週間は終わり |
| On the hard and dirty seat of the train, | 汽車の堅い，汚い座席でまた， |
| I thought again of what I had seen and felt. | 見たり感じたりしたことを考えました。 |
| When I arrived in Calcutta, | カルカッタに着いたとき |
| I was struck by the run-down look of many of the houses. | 驚きました多くの家々の荒廃した外観に。 |

## §4　芸能ウィスパリング通訳

質問はウィスパリング同時通訳で英語に，応答は逐次通訳で日本語に変換して下さい。難しいと思うときは初見で通訳する必要はありません。対訳で学習してからトライして下さい。（テープには英文のみが録音されております）

2-37

**Q1** あなたはハリウッドの謎の一つであると言われていますが，それはどういう意味なのですか。

**A** It means when there were so many idols who failed to continue and disappeared, I have managed to remain in this business.

**Q2** 子役から大人の女優への成長期はどんなだったのですか。

**A** At first I was too busy seeking the reason of my existence to do anything. Not many human beings know who they are or what they really want. Till I controled this identity crisis I could not see things well.

**Q3** どのようにして映画界に入ったのですか。

**A** In my early teens I was so impressed by an excellent movie and decided to be an actress. And I took acting lessons and made my debut when I was 17. At the same time I started to be bullied in school. As I stood out working as an actress, I looked too smart, I guess.

**Q4** ところで生まれはどこですか。

**A** In a town near San Francisco. I'm the third child of 4.
　Both of my parents were in writing and video production work, we were poor. But fortunately I have been supported by my parents' love. Therefore I have been able to dedicate myself to my profession as an actress.

### 芸能ウィスパリング通訳

　　　　デビューから10年，27歳の若きベテランが明かす，これまでとこれからの自分。アイドル女優から豊かな演技力でオスカーに二度ノミネートされる実力派になった彼女にも精神的葛藤があった。新作"ピンピネラ"の話題を含め，カルラ・ハーレーが過去と現在の自分を語ってくれた。

**Q1** They say you are one of the wonders in Hollywood. What does it mean?

**A** それは多くのアイドルが挫折して消えていくのに私がこの世界に居残れたからだと思います。

**Q2** How were you in the transition from a child-actress to a grown-up actress.

**A** 私は最初，自分の存在理由を探すのに精一杯だったわ。人間て自分は誰なのかとか本当に欲しいものは何なのかなんてわかってる人は少ないのよね。このアイデンティティの危機を制するまでは何もよく見えない状態だったの。

**Q3** How did you go into this motion picture business?

**A** 10代初めにテレビで見た名作映画に感動して女優になろうと決めたの。そして演劇レッスンをうけて17歳でデビューしたの。でもそれと同時に学校でいじめにあうようになったの。女優という目立つ職業のために生意気だと思われたんでしょうね。

**Q4** By the way, where were you born?

**A** サンフランシスコの近くの町よ。4人兄妹の3番目なの。両親とも文筆業やビデオ制作に携わっていたけれど，生活は貧しかったの。でも幸運なことに私は両親の深い愛に支えられてここまで来たわ。それで女優業に打ち込むことができたの。

**Q5** 趣味は切手の収集だそうですね。

**A** No. It's not a hobby. I gather old stamps to send to an organization. And they auction them to use the proceeds for the people in need. I have led a very humble life, without electricity. At that time, the only luxury I had was to eat doughnuts on weekends.

**Q6** 今回の映画のこの役を得るのにライガー監督に売りこんだというのは本当ですか。

**A** (Giggle.) That's right. At the Oscar awards I declared to him that I'm good at playing a role of strong woman.

**Q7** 作品のテーマと役柄に関してはどうでしたか。

**A** It was very hard. The theme was about an ordinary woman involved in a criminal case and in the process of justifying herself, she gets crazed. This type of things can happen in any age, when a cog slips in a machine, you know. It was a part worth working hard.

**Q8** 次作はシリーズの5作目ですが、あなたにとってははじめてのSF作品ですね。あなたはロボットの役だそうですが、その内容は？

**A** I should not tell you about details. If I may say anything it's emphasis is on SF rather than on actions. I was very happy when I got this part. Because this has given me a greater possibility.

**Q9** あなたの将来の展望は

**A** As for now, I have been stable, although I don't think I have found what I really want to do, in these 10 years. So I want to pursue my potentiality by playing a variety of roles.

**Q5** I heard your hobby is stamp collecting, isn't it?

**A** いいえ。趣味ではないの。使い古しの切手を集めて，ある団体に送るとそれをオークションで売って恵まれない人達のために役立てることができるの。私，子供のころに電気もない本当に質素な生活を経験したの。当時の唯一の贅沢は週末に食べられるドーナツだけだったのよ。

**Q6** They say you went to Director Lyger to get this role in this movie, is that right?

**A** ふふふ。本当よ。オスカーのときに，私，強い女の役って得意ですって宣言しておいたの。

**Q7** How was the theme of the work and your part?

**A** 難しいかったわ。テーマは普通の女の人が事件に巻込まれの自分を正当化しようとする過程で，狂気にかられていくというものだったの。これはちょっと歯車が狂うといつの時代にもおこりうる現象ね。やり甲斐がある役だったわ。

**Q8** Next one is the 5th in the series, and isn't it your first time to perform in SF movie? I heard you're going to be a robot, and how is the story?

**A** 詳しいことはまだ言えないの。強いて言えばアクションよりSFの部分が強調されるって言うことかしら。役が来たときは嬉しかったわ。私により大きい可能性を与えてくれたんだもの。

**Q9** Please tell us about your future prospect.

**A** まず，今に関して言うと，とても安定しているわ。この10年で自分の求めるものが見つかったとは言えないけれど。だからまだ色々な役を演じて可能性を追求してみたいわ。

# Lesson 19

## §1 クイック・レスポンス

(1) ボキャビル

**演習方法**

英語と日本語の合成語を2秒以内で発音します。
次に日本語から英語,英語から日本語へ即時変換して下さい。

## Business & Calcutta 2

| | | |
|---|---|---|
| 1 | property | 財産 |
| 2 | deposit | 預ける |
| 3 | withdraw | 引き出す |
| 4 | income tax | 所得税 |
| 5 | endorse | 裏書きする |
| 6 | exchange rate | 為替レート |
| 7 | speculation | 投機 |
| 8 | investment | 投資 |
| 9 | fiscal | 財政上の |
| 10 | economic | 経済の |
| 11 | asset | 資産 |
| 12 | property tax | 財産税 |
| 13 | drawback | 欠点 |
| 14 | survive | 生き残る |
| 15 | abundance | 豊富さ |
| 16 | craftsmen | 職人 |
| 17 | incense | お香 |
| 18 | devotion | 敬神 |
| 19 | varied | 様々で |
| 20 | numerous | 多大な |

(2) **数字**　英語に変換して下さい。

1億，18億，300億，3150億，2000億，4000億，1兆，
3兆，15兆，60兆，100兆，　1000兆，3000億，3500億，
1兆，5000億，　1兆5000億，　2兆4000億，16兆1600億

## §2　リテンションとリプロダクション

(1) **リテンション練習**
数回音読して暗唱して下さい。　　　　　　　　2-38

A　I heard there're more drawbacks in the previous model.
B　Right, the running costs were too high and the design wasn't so good either.
A　Then what were the strengths?
B　The compactness and the price, I guess.
A　I see, how was the energy efficiency?

(2) **リプロダクション**
日本語文を読み，または聞き，即時に訳出して下さい。

A　聞くところによると以前のモデルには欠点があったそうですね。
B　そうです。運転費がかかり過ぎデザインもそんなに良くなかったのです。
A　では何が長所だったのですか？
B　コンパクトなことと価格です。
A　なるほど，エネルギー効率はどうでした？

## §3 区切り聞き

**演習方法**

初回は区切り聞きでリピーティング，二回目は該当部の日本語訳を音読して下さい。三回目は自分の言葉で通訳して下さい。

### Calcutta 2

2-39

| | |
|---|---|
| Calcutta is known for its beggars and poverty. | カルカッタは乞食と貧困で知られています。 |
| Mother Teresa's work has let the world know that, | マザー・テレサの事業でその事実が世界に知れました， |
| there is a lot of sickness and disease there. | 多くの病気があります。 |
| People managed to survive despite the poverty | 人々はやっと生き貧困にもかかわらず |
| and had to accept what life had given them. | 生活が彼等に与えたものを受け入れなければなりませんでした。 |
| Life just went on. | 生活は続きました。 |
| At the ashram, | アシュラムでは |
| there was talk of inner peace | 内的平和と |
| and a new, just society, | 新しい，正義の社会の話があり |
| while in the city | 都市では |
| there were people sleeping | 人々が |
| on the sidewalks. | 歩道に寝ていました。 |
| Poverty was not the only thing I saw. | 貧困だけを見たのではありません。 |
| There were plenty of smiles and happy faces. | 多くの微笑みや幸せそうな顔がありました。 |

| | |
|---|---|
| There were laughs and there were jokes. | 笑いも冗談もありました。 |
| Everywhere, children smiled at me and asked to have their picture taken. | どこでも子供達は私に微笑んで写真を撮ってくれと言いました。 |
| With my hand on camera button, I couldn't help but notice the abundance of healthy, white teeth behind the huge smiles. | カメラのシャッターに指を置き否応無しに気付いたのは健康な真白い歯が大きな微笑みの中に見えたからです。 |
| Their faces were radiant with laughter and they seemed so full of energy. | 彼等の顔は笑いで輝き彼等は元気一杯でした。 |
| There was also mystery. | 不思議なこともありました。 |
| There were the sounds of Indian music that seemed to lift you into the sky, towards mysteries of life. | インド音楽の音は人を空に上げるようです人生の不思議に向ってです。 |
| There was the splendid work of craftsmen who worked so keenly and slowly. | 素晴らしい仕事がありました。職人によるもので，その人は熱心にゆっくりと働きました。 |
| There was the sweet smell of incense that suggested a culture so rich and old. | お香の甘い香りで思ったことは豊かで古い文化のことでした。 |
| It was a culture where devotion was strong and religious festivals were varied and numerous. | 文化敬神が強く宗教的お祭りが様々で多大にある文化でした。 |

## §4　芸能ウィスパリング通訳

質問はウィスパリング同時通訳で英語に，応答は逐次通訳で日本語に変換して下さい。難しい時は対訳で学習してからトライして下さい。(CDには英文のみが録音されております)　　　　　2-40

**Q1** 新しいレコーディング・スタジオにレコード会社を移籍した経緯を教えて下さい。

**A** The company we have worked with so far is a small scale one and there were operational problems. And we felt we couldn't work as freely as we wished to. Also, we thought it interesting to produce concentrating on the Japanese market. At that time we received a very nice offer from the Stardom Company of Japan and we decided to transfer right away.

**Q2** 契約のトラブルはよくある問題ですが，ビジネスとして金銭問題が絡むと音楽がいやになってしまうことなどはありませんでしたか。

**A** Fortunately we haven't gotten that far. But we have tried not to be deeply involved in business. I think we lose a lot when we think of money.

**Q3** 素晴らしい音楽を作っているのに世間から評価されてないと感じたことはありませんか。

**A** I guess I cannot say anything about that. We haven't had enough opportunities in Europe to appeal to the people. But if we are given chances, I'm sure we can do well.

**Q4** ニュー・アルバムの"ルチャ"というタイトルにはどのような意味が込められているのですか。

**A** Anyway, go for broke. You try and you may get negative reactions. But keep your confidence and advance. That's the message in it.

### 芸能ウィスパリング通訳

　過去3作で確固たる地位を築き，日本のファンにとって大切なバンドとなったアクエリアス。魂の震えを繊細に描写する最新作"ルチャ"発表に併せ緊急インタビュー。バンドのエモーション面を担うハード・ロック・シンガーのビクター R. サンタナに直撃。

**Q1** Would you tell us why and how you move to a new recording studio?

**A** 今までの会社は小規模である上にオペレーション上に問題があったので僕達の自由に活動できないと感じたんだ。それに日本のマーケットに集中して曲を作ってみるのも面白いと思ったんだよ。そんな時，日本のスターダム社からの好意的なオファーを受けてすぐ移籍する気になったんだ。

**Q2** We often hear about contract problems, but when financial problems are involved in business, don't you ever feel disgusted or feel tired of music?

**A** 幸い僕たちはまだそこまでいってないね。でもあまりビジネスには深入りしないようにしている。金のことを考えると音楽は絶対駄目になると思うんだ。

**Q3** Have you ever felt that you haven't been appreciated by the public as you ought to have been, since you have produced wonderful music?

**A** 何とも言えないな。ヨーロッパではリスナーにアピールする場があまり与えられてなっかたんだ。でもそのチャンスが与えられればうまく行くと思っている。

**Q4** Let me ask about your new album "Lucha", what does that title imply?

**A** とにかく当たって砕けろ，トライしてみて反応がネガティブでも自分の信念をもって前進しろというメッセージが込められている。

**Q5** 今回のアルバムの仕上がりには満足していますか。

A  Yes, all of us have tried our best and made a nice album. As for me I could sing naturally, and all the members say this is the best so far.

**Q6** 自己表現の手段としてハード・ロックを選んだのはなぜですか。

A  I happened to love Rock Music when I was a teenager. I like the combination of guitars, drums, bass and singing.

**Q7** 他のメンバーの歌を歌うことで苦労をすることはないですか。

A  To sing other people's songs well is a type of challenge for a vocalist, and to create music making efforts together is great fun although it can be hard. All the words in the songs are so impressive that I could sing them from the bottom of my heart.

**Q8** ミュージシャンとして自分のサウンドを作り続けるのにはハードだと思うのですが，精神面について話して下さい。

A  Music has power which cannot be described with words. When one keeps confidence and does one's best, some time in the future one will be appreciated. This is what I believe 100% and never doubt.

**Q9** これからのバンドの方向性についてはどうでしょうか。

A  We work together to create wonderful things. We try hard to sing songs which are natural and vehement.

**Q10** 日本のファンに何かメッセージがありますか。

A  We have been very grateful to Japanese fans for their support. We hope to keep on creating songs without any compromise. In the end we hope all of you follow the course each chose keeping yourself confident.

**Q5** Are you satisfied at the results in your album?

**A** うん，全員がベストを尽くして良いアルバムができたと思っている。自分としてはすごく自然に歌えたし，メンバーの皆も今までに一番いい出来だと言っている。

**Q6** Why did you choose hard rock as a means to express yourself?

**A** ティーンエイジャーの頃ロックが好きになったんだ。ギターとドラムとベースとボーカルのコンビが好きなんだ。

**Q7** Don't you have any difficulty in singing songs created by other members?

**A** 他人の曲を歌いこなすのはボーカリストにとって一種のチャレンジだし，皆で力をあわせて創作するのは苦労もあるが楽しさも大きいよ。歌詞はどれも共感出来るものばかりだから心をこめて歌えた。

**Q8** For a musician to keep producing one's own sound may be quite hard, I think. Please tell us something about mental aspects.

**A** 音楽は言葉では表現出来ないパワーを持っている。自分を信じてベストを尽くせばいつかは認められると僕は100％信じて疑わない。

**Q9** What is the course for your band to take for the future.

**A** 皆で力を合わせて素晴らしいものをつくっていくよ。僕たちは自然で強烈な歌を歌って行くことを心掛けるつもりだよ。

**Q10** Do you have any message for Japanese fans?

**A** 日本のファンの支援にはすごく感謝している。これからも妥協しない音楽創作を続けていきたいと思っている。最後に，皆も自分の選んだ道を信念を持って進んでもらいたいと願っているよ。

# Lesson 20

## §1 クイック・レスポンス

(1) ボキャビル

**演習方法**

英語と日本語の合成語を2秒以内で発音します。
次に日本語から英語，英語から日本語へ即時変換して下さい。

## Arts & Calcutta 3

| | | |
|---|---|---|
| 1 | backdrop | 背景幕 |
| 2 | costume | 衣装 |
| 3 | property | 大道具 |
| 4 | stage | 舞台 |
| 5 | background | 背景 |
| 6 | play a part | 役割を演じる |
| 7 | impersonate | 役を勤める |
| 8 | direct | 監督する |
| 9 | shoot | 撮影する |
| 10 | perform | 演じる |
| 11 | leading actor | 主役 |
| 12 | stunt | スタント |
| 13 | improvise | 即座に作る |
| 14 | sound effects | 音響効果 |
| 15 | villain | 悪者 |
| 16 | heroin | ヒロイン |
| 17 | hero | ヒーロー |
| 18 | cremation | 火葬 |
| 19 | contemplation | 瞑想 |
| 20 | injustice | 不公平 |

(2) **数字**　英語に変換して下さい。

10億，80億，100億，150億，500億，1000億，2000億，
5000億，6000億，1兆，3兆，15兆，60兆，100兆，25億，
3000億，3500億，2兆4000億，2兆4000億，3兆4000億，
5兆，5000億，5兆5000億，11兆，100兆，1000兆，200万

## §2　リテンションとリプロダクション

### (1)　**リテンション練習**
数回音読して暗唱して下さい。　　　　　　　　🅒 2-41

A　You look a little down these days.
B　Well I'm sick and tired of my present job.
　　I don't think I'm in the right kind of work.
A　Maybe you ought to talk to your section chief.
B　Yeah. I'll do that because I'm thinking of turning in a request for a transfer to another section.
A　I'm sure you can find a section more suited to you.

### (2)　**リプロダクション**
日本語文を読み，または聞き，即時に訳出して下さい。

A　この頃あまり元気がないようですね。
B　今の仕事でうんざりしているのです。
　　自分に合った仕事についていると思えないのです。
A　課長に話してみるべきですよ
B　ええ，そうします。他の課に転任する希望を出そうと思っていますので。
A　きっと，もっとあなたに合った課が見つかりますよ。

## §3 区切り聞き

**演習方法**

初回は区切り聞きでリピーティング，二回目は該当部の日本語訳を音読して下さい。三回目から自分の言葉で通訳して下さい。

## Calcutta 3　　　　　2-42

| | |
|---|---|
| Life is always full of struggle | 人生は苦悩で一杯ですが |
| but I believe that it is | 私の考えでは， |
| these struggles | これらの苦悩で |
| that give meaning to life. | 人生に意味ができるのです。 |
| And we all have something | そして，私達全員が何か |
| different to learn from life. | 違ったものを人生から学ぶのです。 |
| | |
| On one of my last nights in Calcutta, | カルカッタ滞在も終わろうとするある晩， |
| I visited a local crematorium | 現地の火葬場に |
| with some friends and | 友達と行き |
| saw the burning of an old man. | 老人の火葬を見ました。 |
| My thoughts were of death and life. | 私は生と死を考えました。 |
| Life is so fragile. | 生命はもろいのです。 |
| So, what was I going to do with my life? | 私は自分の人生で何をするのでしょう？ |
| I was young and eager to seek more. | 私は若く熱心にもっと求めていました。 |
| My thoughts were stopped. | 思考が止まりました。 |
| There was constant chattering. | 絶え間ない話し声がありました。 |
| From down the streets, | 通りのずっと向こうの方から |
| a mysterious sound could | 不思議な音楽が |

| | |
|---|---|
| barely be heard. | わずかに聞こえました。 |
| As the horns and drums became louder and closer, | ラッパと太鼓の音が段々大きくなり |
| it became clear that a festival was approaching. | はっきりとわかりましたお祭りがやって来るのが。 |
| The people became more animated and the music became overwhelming. | 人々はより活気づき音楽は圧倒的になりました。 |
| It was then at that moment that the magic of Calcutta became so apparent. | この瞬間カルカッタの魔法がはっきりしました。 |
| The richness of music, the beauty of celebrations and the wonder of people deeply involved in life. | 音楽の豊かさお祝いの美しさ人々の不思議さが人生に関係していたのです。 |
| Life wasn't a shiny pearl all the time but there were times when the pearl of life shone and revealed its absolute brilliance. | 人生は常に輝く真珠であるわけではありませんがそういう時もあったのです人生の真珠が輝き完全な輝きを現した時も。 |
| These were the moments that made life extremely special. These were the moments we lived for. | その瞬間人生は本当に特別になります。私達はそれを求めていきているのです。 |

## §4 ウィスパリング芸能通訳

質問はウィスパリング同時通訳で英語に，応答は逐次通訳で日本語に変換して下さい。難しいときは対訳で学習してからトライして下さい。
(テープには英文のみが録音されております) 2-43

**Q1** 2月のオランダでのフリーファイト興業ではタイトル戦ではありませんでしたが，チャンピオンのニーマンと引き分けましたね。次はタイトルを狙っていくのですか。

**A** Well, yes. It's a shame the bout didn't finish in the satisfactory form. Next time I'm going to show how good Hasdel is.

**Q2** 普段のトレーニングの内容はどういうものですか。

**A** Kick boxing, Sambo, Amateur wrestling, Muway Thai, Power lifting are included on my comprehensive training menu.

**Q3** 次回の日本大会出場が決まりましたね。あなたにとっては待望の日本での試合となるわけですが。

**A** I myself am always ready to go to Japan. I'll try hard to satisfy the Japanese fans. If they give me a chance, I bet I will be one of the contenders for the top rank. Look forward to seeing me.

**Q4** 対戦相手はまだ未発表ですが，試合はどのように運んでいかれるのですか。

**A** I don't want to talk about my strategies so much. But let me tell you I have ample preliminary knowledge about other athletes.

**Q5** どんな選手をターゲットにしたいですか。

**A** All the Japanese athletes. Their fighting styles are good to cope with all types of situations and the varieties of techniques are something. If there's a chance I want to fight against Nagasaki to get even with him.

## スポーツ通訳　ウィスパリング

何かと話題を呼んだ今オランダ大会。次回への参戦も決定しさらに練習にも熱が入る格闘家ハスデルを直撃。

**Q1** At the Free Fight competition held in Holland last February, although it was not for the title you and Nieman, the champion ended in a draw. Are you going after the title next time?

**A** うん，そうだな。この前は中途半端な形で終わって残念だった。次はファスデルが何者かを見せられるだろう。

**Q2** What do you do in your regular training.

**A** キック・ボクシング，サンボ，アマレス，ムエタイ，パワーリフティングなど総合的なメニューで練習している。

**Q3** Your entry in the next competition in Japan has been decided. I think you have always wanted to participate in matches in Japan.

**A** 俺自身はいつでも日本に行く用意はできている。日本のファンに満足してもらえるファイトを心掛けるよ。チャンスが与えられればきっとトップ争いに入って見せる。期待していてくれ。

**Q4** Your opponent hasn't been announced yet, but how are you planning to proceed the match itself.

**A** 戦略についてはあまり話したくないな。しかし他の選手達についての予備知識は十分あるとだけ言っておこう。

**Q5** Which athletes are you targeting?

**A** 日本人選手は全員だ。彼等のオール・ラウンドな戦い，テクニックの豊富さには尊敬すべきものがある。もしチャンスがあれば長崎と戦い，借りを返したい。

**Q6** メンタル面ではどのようなトレーニングをしているのですか。

**A** Every morning and night, I have been doing image training, so that I never fall.

**Q7** 今回のスパーリングをみたところ，関節技と締め技を中心に試合を組み立てていましたね。

**A** Yes. When I fight against an athlete larger than me, I think joint reversing will be the finishing technique. Although my basic training is done through kick-boxing, I have learned Sambo and free style wrestling seriously and I think those have given me more variations in my fighting style.

**Q8** 今現在のコンディッションはどうですか。

**A** Very good. I have gained 10 kilos but this has turned out favorably and now I can kick more sharply.

**Q9** ウエイトを上げるのは新しいアドバイザーの指示ですか。

**A** That's right. I have been lucky to get a good adviser and a good coach, this time. Thanks to them, I could shape myself up in a very excellent condition.

**Q10** 最後にファンの皆さんに一言どうぞ。

**A** I want the fans to see my real strength. I'm going to have a good result in Japan, so look forward to it.

**Q6** In terms of mental conditioning, what type of training have you been doing?

**A** 俺は毎日朝と晩に絶対に倒れないためのイメージ・トレーニングを実行している。

**Q7** Observing your sparring this time, I think you have organized your strategy centering joint reversing techniques and strangleholds, right?

**A** うん。自分より大きい選手と戦うには，関節技が決め手になると思うんだ。俺はキック・ボクシングがベースだがサンボやフリースタイルレスリングも真剣に学んで戦い方に幅が出たと思う。

**Q8** How is your condition now?

**A** 非常にいい，ウエイトを10キロつけたがかえって蹴りに切れがでてきて喜んでいる。

**Q9** As for increasing your weight, is it the suggestion from your new adviser?

**A** そうだ。今回はいいアドバイザーとコーチに恵まれてラッキーだ，彼等のおかげで自分を非常にいいコンディッションにしあげられたんだ。

**Q10** The last thing to ask you, any word for the fans?

**A** ファンの皆に俺のリアルな強さを見てほしい。日本では絶対にいい結果を出して見せるから期待していてくれ。

## 一語遅れ通訳練習　ウォーミング・アップ　単文

| | | |
|---|---|---|
| 1 | After you. | お先にどうぞ |
| 2 | Die hard. | なかなかなくならない |
| 3 | Couldn't be! | まさか |
| 4 | Cash or charge? | 現金？　クレジット？ |
| 5 | Good timing. | グッドタイミング |
| 6 | How did you know? | どうしてわかったの？ |
| 7 | I have no idea. | 見当が付きません |
| 8 | Shoot. | ちぇ |
| 9 | It's a small world. | 世間は狭いですね |
| 10 | It's not urgent. | 急ぎではありません |
| 11 | Never mind. | 気にするな |
| 12 | No kidding. | 冗談でしょう |
| 13 | Who's calling, Please? | どなた様ですか |
| 14 | Think nothing of it. | どう致しまして |
| 15 | I'm all thumbs. | 私は不器用です |
| 16 | I'm all ears. | 熱心に聞いています |
| 17 | Give me a rain check. | またにしてよ |
| 18 | What a coincidence. | 何という偶然 |
| 19 | That sounds nice. | いいですね |
| 20 | You never know. | さてどうだか |
| 21 | I overslept. | 寝過ごした |
| 22 | I feel dizzy. | 目まいがする |
| 23 | Feel free to ask. | 何でも聞いて下さい |
| 24 | This is for you. | これどうぞ |
| 25 | Get the job done. | 仕事を済ませろ |
| 26 | I'm depressed. | 気が滅入っています |
| 27 | It's up to you. | あなた次第です |
| 28 | So much for today. | 今日はここまで |
| 29 | Give me a break. | 勘弁してよ |

| | | |
|---|---|---|
| 30 | Take my word for it. | 本当ですよ |
| 31 | Absolutely. | 絶対に |
| 32 | By no means. | だめ |
| 33 | Hurry. | 急いで |
| 34 | Take care. | 気をつけて |
| 35 | Watch out. | 注意して |
| 36 | No way. | 絶対駄目です |
| 37 | Open sesame. | 開け胡麻 |
| 38 | What a jerk. | 嫌な奴 |
| 39 | I'll see to it. | 取り計らいます |
| 40 | Take it easy. | 呑気にやろう |
| 41 | Come on. | いいでしょう |
| 42 | No problem. | 問題ない |
| 43 | Shame on you. | 恥を知れ |
| 44 | By the way | ところで |
| 45 | Incidentally | ちなみに |
| 46 | Good grief. | あーあ |
| 47 | Anyway. | とにかく |
| 48 | How about wine? | ワインはどう？ |
| 49 | Out of the blue. | だしぬけに |
| 50 | Which is which? | どっちがどっち |
| 51 | What page? | 何ページですか |
| 52 | What's today? | 今日は何曜日？ |
| 53 | I'll do that. | そうします |
| 54 | Have fun. | 楽しんできて |
| 55 | I goofed. | 失敗した |
| 56 | I'm tied up. | 手が離せません |
| 57 | About the same. | 相変わらずです |
| 58 | Get set, go. | 用意ドン |
| 59 | What a mess. | 何てことだ |
| 60 | It hurts. | 痛みます |
| 61 | Are you free tonight? | 今晩暇ですか |

| | | |
|---|---|---|
| 62 | I couldn't care less. | 全然構わない |
| 63 | What's the material? | 素材は何ですか |
| 64 | First things first. | 重要な事から先に |
| 65 | Out of the question. | 問題外です |
| 66 | It doesn't make sense. | 理屈にあわない |
| 67 | Not bad. | なかなかいいですね |
| 68 | I'm not in the mood. | その気になれない |
| 69 | Couldn't be better. | 最高です |
| 70 | Speak of the devil. | 噂をすれば影 |
| 71 | Have one. | お一つどうぞ |
| 72 | I have a headache. | 頭が痛い |
| 73 | What do you mean? | どういう事ですか |
| 74 | Is this seat taken? | 空いてますか |
| 75 | I can't hear you. | 聞こえません |
| 76 | I have chills. | 寒気がする |
| 77 | I'm full. | お腹がいっぱいです |
| 78 | As you like. | お好きなように |
| 79 | What a nuisance. | 何と迷惑なことだ |
| 80 | Give it a try. | やってみよう |
| 81 | You took me wrong. | 誤解だよ |
| 82 | That reminds me. | それで思い出した |
| 83 | Looks that way. | そのようですね |
| 84 | Leave it to me. | 私にまかせて下さい |
| 85 | I'd appreciate it. | 宜しくお願い致します |
| 86 | Not on your life. | 絶対に駄目 |
| 87 | Let's take a vote. | 投票しましょう |
| 88 | Sorry to bother you. | 恐縮です |
| 89 | He's history. | 彼は過去の人だ |
| 90 | It's the opposite. | それとは反対です |
| 91 | Never say die. | 諦めないで |
| 92 | I feel for you. | 気の毒に |
| 93 | Right on. | ドンピシャ |

| | | |
|---|---|---|
| 94 | There you go. | そうそう |
| 95 | Sure thing. | もちろん |
| 96 | Way to go. | その調子です |
| 97 | Time is up. | 時間終了です |
| 98 | Hang in there. | 頑張って |
| 99 | Any progress? | 順調？ |
| 100 | Search me. | 知らないよ |
| 101 | Says who? | よく言うよ |
| 102 | He is a nut. | 彼は変わり者だ |
| 103 | I blew it. | へまをした |
| 104 | We're leaving. | 出発します |
| 105 | Don't be silly. | とんでもない |
| 106 | It's my turn. | 私の番です |
| 107 | I'll get it. | 私が受けます |
| 108 | Let's go Dutch. | 割り勘にしよう |
| 109 | Get lost. | 失せろ |
| 110 | Duck! | 身をかがめろ |
| 111 | Look out! | 危ない |
| 112 | Freeze. | 動くな |
| 113 | Any objection? | 異議はありますか |
| 114 | Well done. | でかした |
| 115 | Heads or tails? | 表？裏？ |
| 116 | I'm starving. | 腹ペコだ |
| 117 | Just my luck. | ついてない |
| 118 | If you insist. | 是非と言うのなら |
| 119 | Go to it. | やってみな |
| 120 | Let's face it. | ずばり言って |
| 121 | Take it or leave it. | 嫌なら結構ですよ |
| 122 | I won't be in today. | 今日は休みます |
| 123 | I'll sleep on it. | 一晩よく考える |
| 124 | What do you mean? | どういう事でしょう |
| 125 | I needed it yesterday. | 今すぐに |

| | | |
|---|---|---|
| 126 | I'm sort of tired. | ちょっと疲れた |
| 127 | I'll get by somehow. | 何とかなるでしょう |
| 128 | It's anyone's guess. | ちょっとわかりません |
| 129 | I'll count on you. | 頼りにしているよ |
| 130 | I'm stuck. | 行き詰まってしまった |
| 131 | That's about it. | 大体こんなとろこです |
| 132 | I'm getting nowhere. | うまくいってない |
| 133 | Just like that? | 突然な話ですね |
| 134 | Sorry to be late. | 遅くなって御免 |
| 135 | Let's take a rest. | ちょっと休みましょう |
| 136 | I think we're lost. | 道に迷ったみたいだ |
| 137 | You can't miss it. | 必ずわかりますよ |
| 138 | I can't afford it. | 余裕がありません |
| 139 | It's Greek to me. | ちんぷんかんぷんだ |
| 140 | That would be fun. | きっと楽しいよ |
| 141 | What a business. | 厄介な事になった |
| 142 | It's getting late. | もう遅くなりました |
| 143 | Level with me. | 率直に話して下さい |
| 144 | He is a character. | 彼は変わり者だ |
| 145 | What's on tap today? | 今日の予定は何ですか |
| 146 | Wonders never cease. | いやはや驚いた |
| 147 | That's not a point. | それが問題じゃない |
| 148 | I was expecting you. | お待ちしていました |
| 149 | Cat got your tongue? | どうして黙っているの |
| 150 | None of your business. | 余計なお世話だ |
| 151 | Dinner is ready. | 御飯よ |
| 152 | Either will do. | どちらでもいい |
| 153 | I made it. | うまくいった |
| 154 | Let go. | はなせ |
| 155 | I'm all for it. | 大賛成だ |
| 156 | I'll be darned. | 何てこった |
| 157 | A piece of cake. | 簡単 |

|  |  |  |
|---|---|---|
| 158 | Take your time. | 急ぐ必要はない |
| 159 | I can't wait. | それは楽しみだ |
| 160 | Looks familiar. | 見覚えがある |
| 161 | It's obvious. | 明らかです |
| 162 | I'm beat. | へとへとだ |
| 163 | It's reassuring. | 心強いですね |
| 164 | Suit yourself. | 勝手にしろ |
| 165 | I'll be tempted. | 断れないな |
| 166 | That's terrific. | 素晴らしい |
| 167 | I guarantee it. | 保証します |
| 168 | You've got me. | してやられました |
| 169 | I'm bored. | つまらない |
| 170 | Good for you. | さすが |
| 171 | Who knows? | だれが知るものか |
| 172 | That does it. | 頭にきた |
| 173 | Nothing to it. | 簡単だよ |
| 174 | Look who's here. | これはこれは |
| 175 | He's soft nosed. | 考えが甘い |
| 176 | I mean it. | 本気だ |
| 177 | Come again? | もう一度言って |
| 178 | Just the ticket. | それがいい |
| 179 | Are you through? | 終った？ |
| 180 | A hopeless case. | しょうがない人 |
| 181 | Let's give her a hand. | 彼女に拍手を |
| 182 | First come, first served. | 早い者勝ち |
| 183 | I'll get even with him. | 彼に仕返しするぞ |
| 184 | I got a kick out of it. | 楽しんだ |
| 185 | That's a new one on me. | 初耳だ |
| 186 | You can say that again. | 全くその通り |
| 187 | This is only temporary. | 一時的なことです |
| 188 | You say some nice things. | うまい事を言うね |
| 189 | The sooner, the better. | 早ければ早い程よい |

| | | |
|---|---|---|
| 190 | Things are looking up. | 事態が好転しました |
| 191 | We can live with that. | まあ仕方がないですね |
| 192 | Thanks for everything. | いろいろ有り難う |
| 193 | I remember something. | そう言えば |
| 194 | What grade are you in? | 何年生ですか |
| 195 | A little bird told me. | 秘密だよ |
| 196 | We got nice chemistry. | 相性が良い |
| 197 | How do you like Japan? | 日本はどうですか |
| 198 | I couldn't agree less. | 絶対反対だ |
| 199 | It's really something. | たいしたものですね |
| 200 | What if it rains. | 雨が降ったらどうしよう |
| 201 | Prices went up by 5% | 価格が5％上昇しました |
| 202 | I know how you feel. | お気持ちはわかりますよ |
| 203 | Stay tuned. | チャンネルはこのままで |
| 204 | Beats me. | 知ってるわけないでしょう |
| 205 | So far so good. | 今までのところ順調です |
| 206 | That'll be the day. | そんなことはないでしょう |
| 207 | It's your funeral. | そんなことしたら終わりだ |
| 208 | Not that I know of. | 私の知る限りでは違います |
| 209 | I'd better be going. | そろそろお暇しなくては |
| 210 | It can't be helped. | どうしようもないのです |
| 211 | You said it. | その通り |
| 212 | Fair enough. | まあいいでしょう |
| 213 | I'm with you. | 同感です |
| 214 | If necessary. | 必要ならば |
| 215 | Cut it out. | 黙れ |
| 216 | For one thing. | 一つには |
| 217 | In the long run. | 結局 |
| 218 | On the whole. | 全体的には |
| 219 | I doubt it. | そうは思いません |
| 220 | You name it. | 何から何まである |
| 221 | Period. | そうゆうこと |

| | | |
|---|---|---|
| 222 | Read my lips. | よく聞いて |
| 223 | Did you ever! | 意外や意外 |
| 224 | Snap out of it. | 元気を出して |
| 225 | Bingo! | やった |
| 226 | Get up the nerve. | 勇気を出して |
| 227 | Not in the least. | 全然 |
| 228 | That's an insult. | 失敬な |
| 229 | Serves him right. | いい気味だ |
| 230 | Make a memo of it. | メモして |
| 231 | He's on the phone. | 電話中です |
| 232 | This doesn't pay. | 割が合わない |
| 233 | It's frustrating. | イライラする |
| 234 | It's embarrassing. | ばつが悪い |
| 235 | Is it raining out? | 雨ですか |
| 236 | Ghost of a chance. | 無理だ |
| 237 | Bite your tongue. | うるさい |
| 238 | Long time no see. | しばらく |
| 239 | How's the weather? | 天気はどう |
| 240 | The motion carried. | 動議可決 |
| 241 | Thank you for a delightful evening. | 素晴らしい晩でした |
| 242 | It was a pleasure meeting you. | お会い出来て楽しかったです |
| 243 | We'll work something out. | 何か打つ手を考えましょう |
| 244 | Who's responsible for this? | 責任者はだれですか |
| 245 | Do you follow me? | 私の言っている事がおわかりですか |
| 246 | Tomorrow is another day. | 明日は明日の風が吹く |
| 247 | You'll get the hang of it. | すぐコツを摑みますよ |
| 248 | I know what you mean. | おっしゃりたい事はわかります |
| 249 | I have a sweet tooth. | 甘いものが好きです |
| 250 | The chance of a lifetime. | 一生に一度のチャンス |
| 251 | What have you got to lose? | 駄目でもともとです |
| 252 | I'll make do with this. | これで間に合わせよう |
| 253 | Tomorrow never comes. | 明日に延ばしていたら何も出来ない |

| | | |
|---|---|---|
| 254 | Better late than never. | 遅くても来ないよりはまし |
| 255 | Loose socks were in. | ルーズソックスが流行していた |
| 256 | You made a fool out of yourself. | ばかな事をした |
| 257 | Let's call it a day. | 今日はこれで終りにしましょう |
| 258 | I don't have all day. | 一日中時間があるわけではないんだ |
| 259 | Keep up the good work. | その調子で続けて下さい |
| 260 | Whatever turns you on. | それでいいのなら，構わないけど |
| 261 | Let's look at it this way. | このように考えてみましょう |
| 262 | Last but not least. | 最後ですが忘れてはいけないのが |
| 263 | You're wasting my time. | そんな話に興味はない |
| 264 | I won't settle for anything less. | 妥協はしない |
| 265 | One for all, all for one. | 皆で協力して行う |
| 266 | Political memories are short. | 過去の記憶はすぐ忘れてしまう |
| 267 | What is this in regards to? | (電話の)ご用件は何でしょうか |
| 268 | Keep your fingers crossed. | (指を交差させて)願い事が叶うように祈りましょう |
| 269 | Easier said than done. | 言うはやすし行うはかたし |
| 270 | Hear no evil, speak no evil, see no evil. | 見ざる，言わざる，聞かざる |
| 271 | Go for broke. | あたって砕けろ |

## 簡単な同時通訳

テープ・レコーダーを二台用意して下さい。一台の方に問題テープを入れ，もう一台には訳文を被せて吹き込むためのブランク・テープを用意します。二台のスイッチを同時に入れて練習し，後にパフォーマンスをチェックします。

　予備知識：British Hills で開かれるセミナーの開会式で施設の責任者兼セミナー主催者が参加者に挨拶する。

| 同時通訳初級修了条件 | | |
|---|---|---|
| | A＋ | 初見で 80％以上同時通訳できた。 |
| | A | 初見で 70％以上同時通訳できた。 |
| | B | 初見で 60％以上同時通訳できた。 |

### セミナーでの主催者の挨拶　　2-44

　Ladies and Gentlemen, on behalf of the organizers of this seminar at British Hills, I would like to extend our warmest welcome to all of you.

　It has long been known that environment is a very important factor in the study of language or social studies.

　This center offers a perspective into Anglo-Japanese relations that may not be available elsewhere. But because of this harmonious environment, I think you are cushioned from the Culture Shock that would otherwise await you. The atmosphere of this facility is equivalent to that of an English Boarding school but we cater to "students" of all ages. We are confident that you will relax and enjoy the good life here. We hope this seminar will give you an opportunity to make new friends and deepen your friendship with old ones, too.

　Be certain of an interesting and informative stay as well as a few surprises.

## 著者紹介

### 柴田 Vanessa 清美

| | |
|---|---|
| 1969 年 | 横浜共立学園高校　卒業 |
| 1972 年 | U. S. A. カリフォルニア州アズサ・パシフィック大学卒業<br>現代語学部　スペイン語科 |
| 1973 年 | メキシコ国立グアダラハラ大学交換留学コース修了 |
| 1973 年 | ハイメ・バルメス大学院　修士課程卒業　ラテン・アメリカ研究科 |
| 1974 年 | 国際同時通訳者連盟　同時通訳研究科在籍 |
| 1975 年 | 英語通訳ガイド免許取得後<br>フリー英語通訳ガイドとなり現在に至る。 |
| 1976 年 | 神田外語学院　非常勤講師となり現在に至る。<br>主な担当講座　トーイック講座，英検講座，スペイン語講座，通訳入門講座，観光英語講座，通訳ガイド講座 |
| 1986 年 | 荒田翻訳事務所に所属現在に至る。<br>英語通訳ガイド　　行政書士<br>スペイン語通訳ガイド<br>旅程管理者　　無線技師<br>英検面接委員 |

---

実践ゼミ ウィスパリング同時通訳―改訂新版　CD付

2005 年 7 月 11 日　1 刷
2017 年 12 月 7 日　4 刷

著　者　　柴田バネッサ清美
　　　　　　Ⓒ KIFL 1998
発 行 者　　南雲一範
発 行 所　　株式会社　**南雲堂**
　　　　　　東京都新宿区山吹町 361（〒162-0801）
　　　　　　電　話　（03）3268-2384（営業部）
　　　　　　　　　　（03）3268-2387（編集部）
　　　　　　FAX　　（03）3260-5525（営業部）
　　　　　　振替口座　00160-0-46863
印刷所　株式会社啓文堂　　製本所　松村製本所

E-mail　　nanundo@post.email.ne.jp
Printed in Japan　　　　　　　〈検印省略〉
乱丁・落丁本はご面倒ですが小社通販係宛ご送付下さい。
送料小社負担にてお取替えいたします。
ISBN978-4-523-26452-1　C 0082〈1-452〉

**CD付**

## TOEIC®テスト リスニング・パート 攻略

柴田バネッサ／ロバート・ウェスト共著
A5判　定価1,995円（本体1,900円）

◆ スコア別／弱点克服学習法紹介。
◆ ウィーク・ポイントを分析し、リスニング力アップのトレーニングとその効果を詳述。
◆ ビジネス・シチュエーションの会話問題に重点を置いく。
◆ 過去問題を徹底分析し、頻出する基礎問題を明記する。

**CD付**

## TOEIC®テスト英文法攻略

柴田バネッサ／ロバート・ウェスト共著
A5判　定価1,995円（本体1,900円）

◆ スコアアップに即効のある重要着眼点170を掲載。
◆ TOEICのPartV & PartVIの文法、語彙問題を中心に頻出問題の傾向と対策を検討。
◆ 出題頻度の高いものを知ることにより、タイムロスと失点を防止。
◆ 文法を基礎からチェックしたい人、一気に点数アップを狙う人のために全パターンをカバーする340題を用意。
◆ TOEIC用語300を効率的に覚える頻出語リストを用意した。

**南雲堂**